ISSUES ON TRIAL

Hate Crimes

Other Books in the Issues on Trial Series:

Domestic Violence

Juvenile Justice

Medical Rights

Native American Rights

Political Corruption

Pollution

Terrorism

White Collar Crime

ISSUES ON TRIAL

Hate Crimes

Judith Bruce, Book Editor

GREENHAVEN PRESS
A part of Gale, Cengage Learning

GALE
CENGAGE Learning™

Detroit • New York • San Francisco • New Haven, Conn • Waterville, Maine • London

GALE
CENGAGE Learning™

Christine Nasso, *Publisher*
Elizabeth Des Chenes, *Managing Editor*

For more information, contact:
Greenhaven Press
27500 Drake Rd.
Farmington Hills, MI 48331-3535
Or you can visit our Internet site at gale.cengage.com.

Articles in Greenhaven Press anthologies are often edited for length to meet page requirements. In addition, original titles of these works are changed to clearly present the main thesis and to explicitly indicate the author's opinion. Every effort is made to ensure that Greenhaven Press accurately reflects the original intent of the authors. Every effort has been made to trace the owners of copyrighted material.

Cover photograph by David McNew/Getty Images.

LIBRARY OF CONGRESS CATALOGING-IN-PUBLICATION DATA

Hate crimes / Judith Bruce, book editor.
p. cm. -- (Issues on trial)
Includes bibliographical references and index.
ISBN-13: 978-0-7377-4177-3 (hardcover)
1. Hate crimes--United States--Cases. I. Bruce, Judith, 1960-
KF9304.H38 2009
345.73'025--dc22

2008032033

Printed in the United States of America
1 2 3 4 5 6 7 12 11 10 09 08

Contents

Chapter 3: Victims of Gender Violence Cannot Sue Their Attackers in Federal Court

Chapter 4: Affirming States' Rights to Ban Cross Burning Intended to Intimidate

Foreword

The U.S. courts have long served as a battleground for the most highly charged and contentious issues of the time. Divisive matters are often brought into the legal system by activists who feel strongly for their cause and demand an official resolution. Indeed, subjects that give rise to intense emotions or involve closely held religious or moral beliefs lay at the heart of the most polemical court rulings in history. One such case was *Brown v. Board of Education* (1954), which ended racial segregation in schools. Prior to *Brown*, the courts had held that blacks could be forced to use separate facilities as long as these facilities were equal to that of whites.

For years many groups had opposed segregation based on religious, moral, and legal grounds. Educators produced heartfelt testimony that segregated schooling greatly disadvantaged black children. They noted that in comparison to whites, blacks received a substandard education in deplorable conditions. Religious leaders such as Martin Luther King Jr. preached that the harsh treatment of blacks was immoral and unjust. Many involved in civil rights law, such as Thurgood Marshall, called for equal protection of all people under the law, as their study of the Constitution had indicated that segregation was illegal and un-American. Whatever their motivation for ending the practice, and despite the threats they received from segregationists, these ardent activists remained unwavering in their cause.

Those fighting against the integration of schools were mainly white southerners who did not believe that whites and blacks should intermingle. Blacks were subordinate to whites, they maintained, and society had to resist any attempt to break down strict color lines. Some white southerners charged that segregated schooling was *not* hindering blacks' education. For example, Virginia attorney general J. Lindsay Almond asserted, "With the help and the sympathy and the love and respect of the white people of the South, the colored man has risen under that educational process to a place of eminence and respect throughout the nation. It has served him well." So when the Supreme Court ruled against the segregationists in *Brown*, the South responded with vociferous cries of protest. Even government leaders criticized the decision. The governor of Arkansas, Orval Faubus, stated that he would not "be a party to any attempt to force acceptance of change to which the people are so overwhelmingly opposed." Indeed, resistance to integration was so great that when black students arrived at the formerly all-white Central High School in Arkansas, federal troops had to be dispatched to quell a threatening mob of protesters.

Nevertheless, the *Brown* decision was enforced, and the South integrated its schools. In this instance, the Court, while not settling the issue to everyone's satisfaction, functioned as an instrument of progress by forcing a major social change. Historian David Halberstam observes that the *Brown* ruling "deprived segregationist practices of their moral legitimacy.... It was therefore perhaps the single most important moment of the decade, the moment that separated the old order from the new and helped create the tumultuous era just arriving." Considered one of the most important victories for civil rights, *Brown* paved the way for challenges to racial segregation in many areas, including on public buses and in restaurants.

In examining *Brown*, it becomes apparent that the courts play an influential role—and face an arduous challenge—in shaping the debate over emotionally charged social issues. Judges must balance competing interests, keeping in mind the high stakes and intense emotions on both sides. As exemplified by *Brown*, judicial decisions often upset the status quo and initiate significant changes in society. Greenhaven Press's Issues on Trial series captures the controversy surrounding influential court rulings and explores the social ramifications of such decisions from varying perspectives. Each anthology highlights one social issue—such as the death penalty, students' rights, or wartime civil liberties. Each volume then focuses on key historical and contemporary court cases that helped mold the issue as we know it today. The books include a compendium of primary sources—court rulings, dissents, and immediate reactions to the rulings—as well as secondary sources from experts in the field, people involved in the cases, legal analysts, and other commentators opining on the implications and legacy of the chosen cases. An annotated table of contents, an in-depth introduction, and prefaces that overview each case all provide context as readers delve into the topic at hand. To help students fully probe the subject, each volume contains book and periodical bibliographies, a comprehensive index, and a list of organizations to contact. With these features, the Issues on Trial series offers a well-rounded perspective on the courts' role in framing society's thorniest, most impassioned debates.

Introduction

At no time in history have the people of our world offered and enjoyed more tolerance for one another. Yet, hate crimes—crimes motivated by bias or hatred against others because of race, gender, religion, national origin, sexual orientation, or other protected status—continue to rise in frequency and severity well into the new millennium. While Congress, most state governments, and many municipalities have passed legislation to define hate crimes as separate crimes and to augment penalties for crimes committed out of hatred or bias, solutions for ending acts of hatred remain elusive. Meanwhile, the First Amendment, both essential and restrictive, has continued to shape hate crime legislation, judicial review, and law enforcement.

A History of Hate Crimes

The government first attempted to combat racial hate violence after the Civil War. During Reconstruction, renegade southern white supremacists bitter over their defeat in the war, and later the Ku Klux Klan, unleashed a wave of intimidation and violence against the newly freed slaves in the South. The Klan's organized and unrelenting attacks amounted to armed rebellion, seeking to subjugate blacks, curtail their voting, and win the war the Confederate Army could not. The Klan terrorized the South with whippings, lynchings, and other forms of murder. Whether incapable or unwilling, southern states generally failed to prevent anti-black violence, forcing the federal government to respond.

Consequently, Congress passed the "Enforcement Acts," legislation designed to uphold the rights guaranteed by the Fourteenth Amendment (equal protection under the law) and the Thirteenth and Fifteenth Amendments (prohibiting slavery and pledging that the right to vote will not be impeded).

Although Klan activity diminished as a result of the federal action, it surged anew with the turn of the century. Spreading its "reign of terror" beyond the South, the Klan began targeting Jews, Catholics, integrationists, communists, and any group not representative of the Klan's "Invisible Empire." In response, Congress enacted anti-mask laws meant to protect the civil rights and the lives of the targeted groups. Essentially, these laws criminalized disguises and masks in public. By proscribing the anonymity of the Klan's white hoods, the government significantly decreased Klan activities—at least until a new outbreak of violence erupted after World War II.

The civil rights movement of the 1950s and 1960s, along with the Supreme Court decision in *Brown v. Board of Education* in 1954 (desegregating public schools), ignited an explosion of violence—shootings, beatings, stabbings, mutilations, bombings, and cross burnings—particularly by the Ku Klux Klan. Yet the brutality of some southern police, as they attempted to quash the surging civil rights movement, must also be considered a hate crime—even if it was behind the guise of a badge. Ironically, the renegade bigots and strong-armed southern police tactics turned public opinion against white supremacist attitudes in favor of the underdogs in the battle, African Americans such as Martin Luther King Jr., Rosa Parks, Irene Morgan, the Freedom Riders, and the countless marchers and strikers in their struggle for human rights.

In accordance with the self-righteous attitudes of white Protestant males of the Ku Klux Klan and some southern police, the most common profile of a hate-crime offender is a young white male, emboldened by alcohol or drugs; however, the vast majority of these criminals are unaffiliated with any extremist organization and often come from dysfunctional homes. These offenders react with violence to the tensions and conflicts of a society becoming more diverse and more complex. They feel disconnected from their community in the midst of rapid social change. Sparked by a hateful attitude toward one or more minority groups, they gain a sense of importance and belonging when they vandalize or assault their targets of hatred. Moreover, technology has presented hate crime reprobates with another avenue of attack—the Internet. A proliferation of hate crime Web sites has led to alarm over "cyberhate" and "cyberbullying" as methods of harassing victims, spreading hate crime propaganda, and recruiting members into hate groups.

The Constitution

Although the Equal Protection Clause of the Fourteenth Amendment has been cited in matters of hate crime legislation, it is the First Amendment, the guarantee of freedom of speech, which has influenced so profoundly the course of hate crime legislation and court review. The First Amendment and the five freedoms it includes—religion, speech, press, assembly, and petition—are often referred to as freedom of expression. These rights form the foundation of American democratic government, enabling citizens to participate in the process of self-government. Even though First Amendment freedoms are the most important in the Bill of Rights, the First Amendment has spurred the most contention. The First Amendment has not only guaranteed the expression of deeply held convictions, but also has revealed the profound differences among Americans.

Supreme Court rulings have demonstrated the difficulty of determining when hate speech and hate expression warrant the protection of the First Amendment and when they do not. In the High Court's first hate crimes test, *R.A.V. v. City of St. Paul* (1992), the Court invalidated a city ordinance proscribing hate speech and expression because it discriminated based on the content of the speech and imposed special prohibitions on people who express views on disfavored subjects. In 2003, however, the Court in *Virginia v. Black* upheld a state law outlawing cross burning because cross burning in the United

States has historically evoked a distinctly gruesome menace. The Court forged another distinction regarding hate expression in *Wisconsin v. Mitchell* (2003), whereby the Court ruled unanimously that hate violence falls outside the protection of the First Amendment. The Court reasoned that hate crime, especially in the form of conduct, has a broader range of victims—the community—than a single unbiased crime.

Federal Intervention

Since Congress may enact only those laws based on powers enumerated in the Constitution, the question for the Supreme Court in each particular case is whether Congress has exceeded its powers in enacting legislation meant to deter and punish hate crimes.

Successful legislation passed by Congress includes the Civil Rights Act of 1968, which outlawed racial violence against civil rights workers. In 1990, Congress enacted the Hate Crimes Statistics Act (HCSA) to collect data on hate crimes in order to inform Congress and law enforcement officials of trends in hate crime statistics and the psychological impact on victims and their communities. Another positive effort by Congress to combat hate crimes was evidenced by the passage of the Hate Crimes Sentencing Enhancement Act in 1994, the passage of which was due in part to a Supreme Court decision of the previous year in *Wisconsin v. Mitchell.* In that case, the Court ruled that First Amendment freedom of speech rights are not violated by state hate crime penalty enhancement statutes since the Wisconsin law failed to provoke a foreseeable "chilling effect" on freedom of speech in cases of hate-inspired conduct. The Court reasoned that a hate crime against an individual was a crime against society.

Nonetheless, Congress has suffered setbacks in enacting hate crime legislation. In *United States v. Morrison* (2000), the Court ruled that Congress exceeded its constitutional powers in passing the Violence Against Women Act of 1994 (VAWA), which provided a federal civil remedy for victims of gender-motivated violence. Congress had based their power to create the VAWA on the Commerce Clause and the Fourteenth Amendment. The Court ruled, however, that gender violence could not be tied to economic activity or interstate commerce and the Fourteenth Amendment did not give the federal government the right to regulate local crime or private conduct.

In addition, Congress has not been able to pass the proposed Hate Crimes Prevention Act (HCPA), which would extend federal protection to victims of hate crimes based on sexual orientation, gender, or disability and generally provide Congress with broad powers allowing federal intervention in state hate crime matters. Although the legislation was first proposed in 1999, as of June 2008, the House and Senate had yet to vote on the HCPA. Proponents claim that gender-motivated crimes are in fact hate crimes that require federal intervention. If passed, they declare the HCPA would provide the most substantial gain in federal powers against hate crimes in the last twenty years. Critics assert that the Act would unduly interfere with states' rights and would never withstand Supreme Court scrutiny.

While more states are expected to enact hate crime legislation in the coming years, as with Congress, benevolent efforts to punish hate crime and hate speech must not violate the First Amendment. For a hate crime to be punished as such, it must fall outside the umbrella of protection guaranteed by freedom of expression. The conduct must present a true threat even democracy's greatest liberties cannot abide.

CHAPTER 1

Protecting Freedom of Speech When Legislating Hate Crimes

Case Overview

R.A.V. v. City of St. Paul (1992)

In a case regarding the First Amendment's freedom of speech guarantee and a hate speech law, the Supreme Court ruled against a city ordinance that prohibited the display of a symbol which "arouses anger, alarm, or resentment in others on the basis of race, color, creed, religion or gender." Associate Justice Antonin Scalia rendered the decision in a case whereby the accused and other teenagers burned a makeshift cross made of broken chair legs inside the fenced yard of an African American family. While the Justice conceded that cross burning is certainly reprehensible, the city had other avenues by which to prosecute the offenders without relying upon an ordinance that violated freedom of speech rights.

In addressing the content issue of the statute, Justice Scalia ruled that the First Amendment did not permit the city of St. Paul to impose special prohibitions on speakers who express views on disfavored subjects—"content." Governments may not regulate speech or symbols, asserted Justice Scalia, on the basis of favoritism, hostility, or a specific message, despite the fact that prior Court decisions have proscribed a few limited types of speech, such as obscenity and defamation.

Although the decision was unanimous that the city ordinance violated the First Amendment and the right of free speech, Justice Byron White disagreed with the majority opinion by stating that while the city law was overbroad in its attempt to limit hate speech and expression, the city rightfully possessed a compelling governmental interest in restricting hateful and hurtful speech. The Justice also declared that the First Amendment was not meant to protect every utterance and every form of expression. Furthermore, not all hate speech is simply a public debate, as the majority asserted, but often it results in detrimental harm to individuals and to the community. In a separate concurrence Justice Harry Blackmun agreed with Justice White's assessment that the law in question was overbroad. He also stated, however, that he saw no harm in preventing the city from specifically punishing the race-based fighting words that were detrimental to the community. Justice John Paul Stevens, in his concurrence, disagreed with the reasoning in the majority opinion, but likewise agreed that the St. Paul ordinance was overbroad.

R.A.V. v. City of St. Paul was the Supreme Court's first test of a hate crime statute in light of the broad powers of the First Amendment. Yet with three concurrences, lower courts attempted to interpret the ruling and legislatures struggled to find ways to protect minorities and their communities—the victims of hate crime—from the harmful consequences of hate expression. Critics argued that the Court failed to recognize the city's compelling interest in backing a law that protected minority groups from the heinous acts of hate-inspired criminals. Proponents supported the decision as pivotal in the protection of freedom of expression. Eleven years later, *Virginia v. Black* would take up the cross-burning issue once again, with a far different result.

"The point of the First Amendment is that majority preferences must be expressed in some fashion other than silencing speech on the basis of its content."

The Court's Decision: Ordinance Punishing Racist Statements Violates Freedom of Speech

Antonin Scalia

In this unanimous majority opinion, Antonin Scalia explains that in R.A.V. v. St. Paul *the court found that a city ordinance prohibiting the display of a symbol that arouses anger, alarm, or resentment in others based on race, religion, or gender violates the right of free speech under the First Amendment. In this case, teenagers burned a cross inside the fenced yard of an African American family. The Court determined that the law imposed specific prohibitions on people who express views on disfavored subjects including race, religion, and gender. Governments may not regulate speech or symbols, stated the Justice, on the basis of favoritism, hostility, or a specific message, despite the fact that Constitutional law does proscribe a few limited types of speech, such as obscenity and defamation. Scalia concludes that content-based prohibitions violate the right of freedom of speech. Antonin Scalia is a former attorney, professor, and Court of Appeals judge. He was nominated to the Supreme Court by President Ronald Reagan in 1986 and took his place on the bench that year.*

Antonin Scalia, majority opinion, *R.A.V. v. City of St. Paul*, U.S. Supreme Court, 505 U.S. 377, in Legal Information Institute, Cornell University Law School, 1992.

In the predawn hours of June 21, 1990, petitioner [Robert A. Viktora] and several other teenagers allegedly assembled a crudely made cross by taping together broken chair legs. They then allegedly burned the cross inside the fenced yard of a black family that lived across the street from the house where petitioner was staying. Although this conduct could have been punished under any of a number of laws, one of the two provisions under which respondent city of St. Paul chose to charge petitioner (then a juvenile) was the St. Paul Bias-Motivated Crime Ordinance, which provides:

> Whoever places on public or private property a symbol, object, appellation, characterization or graffiti, including, but not limited to, a burning cross or Nazi swastika, which one knows or has reasonable grounds to know arouses anger, alarm or resentment in others on the basis of race, color, creed, religion or gender commits disorderly conduct and shall be guilty of a misdemeanor. . . .

Freedom of Speech Restrictions

The proposition that a particular instance of speech can be proscribable on the basis of one feature (e.g., obscenity) but not on the basis of another (e.g., opposition to the city government) is commonplace, and has found application in many contexts. We have long held, for example, that nonverbal expressive activity can be banned because of the action it entails, but not because of the ideas it expresses—so that burning a flag in violation of an ordinance against outdoor fires could be punishable, whereas burning a flag in violation of an ordinance against dishonoring the flag is not. Similarly, we have upheld reasonable "time, place, or manner" restrictions, but only if they are "justified without reference to the content of the regulated speech" [*Ward v. Rock Against Racism*, 1989]. And just as the power to proscribe particular speech on the basis of a non-content element (e.g., noise) does not entail the power to proscribe the same speech on the basis of a content element, so also the power to proscribe it on the basis of one content element (e.g., obscenity) does not entail the power to proscribe it on the basis of *other* content elements.

In other words, the exclusion of "fighting words" from the scope of the First Amendment simply means that, for purposes of that Amendment, the unprotected features of the words are, despite their verbal character, essentially a "nonspeech" element of communication. Fighting words are thus analogous to a noisy sound truck: each is, as Justice Frankfurter recognized [in *Niemotko v. Maryland*], a "mode of speech," both can be used to convey an idea; but neither has, in and of itself, a claim upon the First Amendment. As with the sound truck, however, so also with fighting words: the government may not regulate use based on hostility—or favoritism—towards the underlying message expressed.

When the basis for the content discrimination consists entirely of the very reason the entire class of speech at issue is proscribable, no significant danger of idea or viewpoint discrimination exists. Such a reason, having been adjudged neutral enough to support exclusion of the entire class of speech from First Amendment protection, is also neutral enough to form the basis of distinction within the class. To illustrate: a State might choose to prohibit only that obscenity which is the most patently offensive in its prurience—i.e., that which involves the most lascivious displays of sexual activity. But it may not prohibit, for example, only that obscenity which includes offensive *political* messages. And the Federal Government can criminalize only those threats of violence that are directed against the President—since the reasons why threats of violence are outside the First Amendment (protecting individuals from the fear of violence, from the disruption that fear engenders, and from the possibility that the threatened violence will occur) have special force when applied to the person of the President. . . .

Secondary Effects of Speech

Another valid basis for according differential treatment to even a content-defined subclass of proscribable speech is that the subclass happens to be associated with particular "secondary effects" of the speech, so that the regulation is [as cited in *Renton v. Playtime Theatres, Inc.*] "*justified* without reference to the content of the . . . speech" (1986). A State could, for example, permit all obscene live performances except those involving minors. Moreover, since words can in some circumstances violate laws directed not against speech, but against conduct (a law against treason, for example, is violated by telling the enemy the nation's defense secrets), a particular content-based subcategory of a proscribable class of speech can be swept up incidentally within the reach of a statute directed at conduct, rather than speech. Thus, for example, sexually derogatory "fighting words," among other words, may produce a violation of Title VII's general prohibition against sexual discrimination in employment practices. Where the government does not target conduct on the basis of its expressive content, acts are not shielded from regulation merely because they express a discriminatory idea or philosophy.

These bases for distinction refute the proposition that the selectivity of the restriction is "even arguably 'conditioned upon the sovereign's agreement with what a speaker may intend to say'" [*Metromedia, Inc. v. San Diego*, 1981]. There may be other such bases as well. Indeed, to validate such selectivity (where totally proscribable speech is at issue), it may not even be necessary to identify any particular "neutral" basis, so long as the nature of the content discrimination is such that there is no realistic possibility that official suppression of ideas is afoot. (We cannot think of any First Amendment interest that would stand in the way of a State's prohibiting only those obscene motion pictures with blue-eyed actresses.) Save for that limitation, the regulation of "fighting words," like the regulation of noisy speech, may address some offensive instances and leave other, equally offensive, instances alone.

Dissecting Ordinance Language

Applying these principles to the St. Paul ordinance, we conclude that, even as narrowly construed by the Minnesota Supreme Court, the ordinance is facially unconstitutional. Although the phrase in the ordinance, "arouses anger, alarm or resentment in others," has been limited by the Minnesota Supreme Court's construction to reach only those symbols or displays that amount to "fighting words," the remaining, unmodified terms make clear that the ordinance applies only to "fighting words" that insult, or provoke violence, "on the basis of race, color, creed, religion or gender." Displays containing abusive invective, no matter how vicious or severe, are permissible unless they are addressed to one of the specified disfavored topics. Those who wish to use "fighting words" in connection with other ideas—to express hostility, for example, on the basis of political affiliation, union membership, or homosexuality—are not covered. The First Amendment does not permit St. Paul to impose special prohibitions on those speakers who express views on disfavored subjects.

In its practical operation, moreover, the ordinance goes even beyond mere content discrimination to actual viewpoint discrimination. Displays containing some words—odious racial epithets, for example—would be prohibited to proponents of all views. But "fighting words" that do not themselves invoke race, color, creed, religion, or gender—aspersions upon a person's mother, for example—would seemingly be usable in the placards of those arguing *in favor* of racial, color, etc. tolerance and equality, but could not be used by that speaker's opponents. One could hold up a sign saying, for example, that all "anti-Catholic bigots" are misbegotten; but not that all "papists" are, for that would insult and provoke violence "on the basis of religion." St. Paul has no such authority to license one side of a debate to fight freestyle, while requiring the other to follow Marquis of Queensbury Rules.

What we have here, it must he emphasized, is not a prohibition of fighting words that are directed at certain persons or groups (which would be *facially* valid if it met the requirements of the Equal Protection Clause); but rather, a prohibition of fighting words that contain (as the Minnesota Supreme Court repeatedly emphasized) messages of "bias-motivated" hatred and, in particular, as applied to this case, messages "based on virulent notions of racial supremacy." One must wholeheartedly agree with the Minnesota Supreme Court that "[i]t is the responsibility, even the obligation, of diverse communities to confront such notions in whatever form they appear," but the manner of that confrontation cannot consist of selective limitations upon speech. St. Paul's brief asserts that a general "fighting words" law would not meet the city's needs, because only a content-specific measure can communicate to minority groups that the "group hatred" aspect of such speech "is not condoned by the majority." The point of the First Amendment is that majority preferences must be expressed in some fashion other than silencing speech on the basis of its content. . . .

Benevolent Censorship Unconstitutional

The content-based discrimination reflected in the St. Paul ordinance comes within neither any of the specific exceptions to the First Amendment prohibition we discussed earlier, nor within a more general exception for content discrimination that does not threaten censorship of ideas. It assuredly does not fall within the exception for content discrimination based on the very reasons why the particular class of speech at issue (here, fighting words) is proscribable. As explained earlier, the reason why fighting words are categorically excluded from the protection of the First Amendment is not that their content communicates any particular idea, but that their content embodies a particularly intolerable (and socially unnecessary) *mode* of expressing *whatever* idea the speaker wishes to convey. St. Paul has not singled out an especially offensive mode of expression—it has not, for example, selected for prohibition only those fighting words that communicate ideas in a threatening (as opposed to a merely obnoxious) manner. Rather, it has proscribed fighting words of whatever manner that communicate messages of racial, gender, or religious intolerance. Selectivity of this sort creates the possibility that the city is seeking to handicap the expression of particular ideas. That possibility would alone be enough to render the ordinance presumptively invalid, but St. Paul's comments and concessions in this case elevate the possibility to a certainty.

Finally, St. Paul and its amici defend the conclusion of the Minnesota Supreme Court that, even if the ordinance regulates expression based on hostility towards its protected ideological content, this discrimination is nonetheless justified because it is narrowly tailored to serve compelling state interests. Specifically, they assert that the ordinance helps to ensure the basic human rights of members of groups that have historically been subjected to discrimination, including the right of such group members to live in peace where they wish. We do not doubt that these interests are compelling, and that the ordinance can be said to promote them. But the "danger of censorship" presented by a facially content-based statute [*Leathers v. Medlock*, 1991], requires that that weapon be employed only where it is "*necessary* to serve the asserted [compelling] interest" [*Burson v. Freeman*, 1992 (emphasis added)]. The existence of adequate content-neutral alternatives thus "undercut[s] significantly" any defense of such a statute [*Boos v. Barry, supra*], casting considerable doubt on the government's protestations that "the asserted justification is in fact an accurate description of the purpose and effect of the law" [*Burson*]. The dispositive question in this case, therefore, is whether content discrimination is reasonably necessary to achieve St.

Paul's compelling interests; it plainly is not. An ordinance not limited to the favored topics, for example, would have precisely the same beneficial effect. In fact, the only interest distinctively served by the content limitation is that of displaying the city council's special hostility towards the particular biases thus singled out. That is precisely what the First Amendment forbids. The politicians of St. Paul are entitled to express that hostility—but not through the means of imposing unique limitations upon speakers who (however benightedly) disagree.

Let there be no mistake about our belief that burning a cross in someone's front yard is reprehensible. But St. Paul has sufficient means at its disposal to prevent such behavior without adding the First Amendment to the fire.

"This case could easily be decided within the contours of established First Amendment law by holding . . . that the St. Paul ordinance is fatally overbroad because it criminalizes not only unprotected expression but expression protected by the First Amendment."

Concurring Opinion: Law's Reach Is Overbroad Under the First Amendment

Byron White

In R.A.V. v. City of St. Paul *the Court found a St. Paul ordinance banning bias-motivated speech in violation of the Constitutional right to free speech. Justice Byron White states in the following concurring opinion that the St. Paul ordinance extended beyond "fighting words" to speech protected by the First Amendment; thus the law's reach was overbroad, criminalizing not only unprotected expression, but also expression protected by the right of freedom of speech. Fighting words are not protected by the First Amendment, the Justice reasons, since the Amendment was not intended to protect every utterance. While the majority opinion considers fighting words a form of "debate," White asserts that not all hate speech should be considered a form of public discussion; accordingly, by protecting fighting words, he asserts, the majority opinion gives fighting words "equal constitutional footing" to political discussion and other socially significant expression. Byron White, a conservative, was appointed to*

Byron White, concurring opinion, *R.A.V. v. City of St. Paul*, U.S. Supreme Court, 505 U.S. 377, in Legal Information Institute, Cornell University Law School, 1992.

the Supreme Court by President John F. Kennedy in 1962. He served for thirty-one years before his retirement in 1993.

I agree with the majority that the judgment of the Minnesota Supreme Court should be reversed. However, our agreement ends there.

This case could easily be decided within the contours of established First Amendment law by holding, as petitioner argues, that the St. Paul [Minnesota] ordinance is fatally overbroad because it criminalizes not only unprotected expression but expression protected by the First Amendment. Instead, "find[ing] it unnecessary" to consider the questions upon which we granted review, Court holds the ordinance facially unconstitutional on a ground that was never presented to the Minnesota Supreme Court, a ground that has not been briefed by the parties before this Court, a ground that requires serious departures from the teaching of prior cases and is inconsistent with the plurality opinion in *Burson v. Freeman* (1992), which was joined by two of the five Justices in the majority in the present case. . . .

Categories of Expressions

This Court's decisions have plainly stated that expression falling within certain limited categories so lacks the values the First Amendment was designed to protect that the Constitution affords no protection to that expression. *Chaplinsky v. New Hampshire* (1942), made the point in the clearest possible terms:

> There are certain well-defined and narrowly limited classes of speech, the prevention and punishment of which have never been thought to raise any Constitutional problem. . . . It has been well observed that such utterances are no essential part of any exposition of ideas, and are of such slight social value as a step to truth that any benefit that may be derived from them is clearly outweighed by the social interest in order and morality.

Thus, as the majority concedes . . . this Court has long held certain discrete categories of expression to be proscribable on the basis of their content. For instance, the Court has held that the individual who falsely shouts "fire" in a crowded theatre may not claim the protection of the First Amendment. The Court has concluded that neither child pornography nor obscenity is protected by the First Amendment. . . .

Fighting Words

It is inconsistent to hold that the government may proscribe an entire category of speech because the content of that speech is evil, but that the government may not treat a subset of that category differently without violating the First Amendment; the content of the subset is, by definition, worthless and undeserving of constitutional protection.

The majority's observation that fighting words are "quite expressive indeed," is no answer. Fighting words are not a means of exchanging views, rallying supporters, or registering a protest; they are directed against individuals to provoke violence or to inflict injury. Therefore, a ban on all fighting words or on a subset of the fighting words category would restrict only the social evil of hate speech, without creating the danger of driving viewpoints from the marketplace.

Therefore, the Court's insistence on inventing its brand of First Amendment underinclusiveness puzzles me. The overbreadth doctrine has the redeeming virtue of attempting to avoid the chilling of protected expression, but the Court's new "underbreadth" creation serves no desirable function. Instead, it permits, indeed invites, the continuation of expressive conduct that, in this case, is evil and worthless in First Amendment terms, until the city of St. Paul cures the underbreadth by adding to its ordinance a catch-all phrase such as "and all other fighting words that may constitutionally be subject to this ordinance."

Any contribution of this holding to First Amendment jurisprudence is surely a negative one, since it necessarily signals that expressions of violence, such as the message of intimidation and racial hatred conveyed by burning a cross on someone's lawn, are of sufficient value to outweigh the social interest in order and morality that has traditionally placed such fighting words outside the First Amendment. Indeed, by characterizing fighting words as a form of "debate," the majority legitimates hate speech as a form of public discussion.

Compelling State Interest

Furthermore, the Court obscures the line between speech that could be regulated freely on the basis of content (i.e., the narrow categories of expression falling outside the First Amendment) and that which could be regulated on the basis of content only upon a showing of a compelling state interest (i.e., all remaining expression). By placing fighting words, which the Court has long held to be valueless, on at least equal constitutional footing with political discourse and other forms of speech that we have deemed to have the greatest social value, the majority devalues the latter category.

In a second break with precedent, the Court refuses to sustain the ordinance even though it would survive under the strict scrutiny applicable to other protected expression. Assuming, *arguendo* [for the sake of argument], that the St. Paul ordinance is a content-based regulation of protected expression, it nevertheless would pass First Amendment review under settled law upon a showing that the regulation "'is necessary to serve a compelling state interest and is narrowly drawn to achieve that end'" [*Simon & Schuster, Inc. v. New York Crime Victims Board*, 1991]. St. Paul has urged that its ordinance, in the words of the majority, "helps to ensure the basic human rights of members of groups that have historically been subjected to discrimination. . . ." The Court expressly concedes that this interest is compelling, and is promoted by the ordinance. Nevertheless, the Court treats strict scrutiny analysis as irrelevant to the constitutionality of the legislation. . . .

Under the majority's view, a narrowly drawn, content-based ordinance could never pass constitutional muster if the object of that legislation could be accomplished by banning a wider category of speech. This appears to be a general renunciation of strict scrutiny review, a fundamental tool of First Amendment analysis. . . .

Overbreadth Doctrine

Although I disagree with the Court's analysis, I do agree with its conclusion: the St. Paul ordinance is unconstitutional. However, I would decide the case on overbreadth grounds.

We have emphasized time and again that overbreadth doctrine is an exception to the established principle that

> a person to whom a statute may constitutionally be applied will not be heard to challenge that statute on the ground that it may conceivably be applied unconstitutionally to others, in other situations not before the Court [*Broadrick v. Oklahoma*, 1973].

A defendant being prosecuted for speech or expressive conduct may challenge the law on its face if it reaches protected expression, even when that person's activities are not protected by the First Amendment. This is because

> the possible harm to society in permitting some unprotected speech to go unpunished is outweighed by the possibility that protected speech of others may be muted [*Broadrick*].

However, we have consistently held that, because overbreadth analysis is "strong medicine," it may be invoked to strike an entire statute only when the overbreadth of the statute is not only "real, but substantial as well, judged in relation to the statute's plainly legitimate sweep" [*Broadrick*], and when the statute is not susceptible to limitation or partial invalidation.

Today, the Court has disregarded two established principles of First Amendment law without providing a coherent replacement theory. Its decision is an arid, doctrinaire interpretation, driven by the frequently irresistible impulse of judges to tinker with the First Amendment. The decision is mischievous at best, and will surely confuse the lower courts. I join the judgment, but not the folly of the opinion.

"The case, R.A.V. v. City of St. Paul, *comes at a time of national debate over hate speech laws and campus speech codes that many conservatives and some liberals see as imposing a regime of 'political correctness.'"*

The Ruling in *R.A.V. v. City of St. Paul* Is Far Reaching

Ruth Marcus

The Court ruled in R.A.V. v. City of St. Paul *that a St. Paul ordinance prohibiting bias-motivated speech was unconstitutional. Writing for the majority, Antonin Scalia declared that a law may not prohibit speech or expression based on its content. Although the decision was unanimous, four Justices disagreed with the reasoning of the majority. In this viewpoint, Ruth Marcus reports that states and civil rights groups were divided in their views on the ruling; their concern involved the effect on other similar laws, the urge to punish hate crimes, and the guarantee of freedom of speech. She relays the concerns of many that the court ruling may have far-reaching consequences. Marcus concludes that the Court's split reasoning, which included three concurrences, leaves future judicial decisions in doubt. Ruth Marcus is a reporter for* The Washington Post.

[On June 22, 1992,] the Supreme Court unanimously struck down a St. Paul, Minn., hate crimes law, casting doubt on the constitutionality of scores of other state and local laws and on campus speech codes that punish students for offensive remarks.

Ruth Marcus, "Supreme Court Overturns Law Barring Hate Crimes; Free Speech Ruling Seen as Far-Reaching," *Washington Post*, June 23, 1992. Reprinted with permission.

The court was united in its conclusion that the St. Paul ordinance, which included a restriction on cross burning and swastika displays, violated freedom of speech. But the justices were bitterly divided in their reasoning.

The five-justice majority, led by Antonin Scalia, adopted a far-reaching approach that experts said might be used to invalidate other laws that prohibit cross burning—in place in 15 states and the District—or to strike down other statutes that impose stiffer penalties on crimes such as vandalism, arson and assault when they are motivated by racial, religious or other bias.

Protecting Freedom of Speech

In its zeal to show minority groups that it abhors prejudice, Scalia said, government is not allowed to selectively silence speech on the basis of its content.

Four justices—Byron R. White, Harry A. Blackmun, Sandra Day O'Connor and John Paul Stevens—agreed with the result but blasted the majority's reasoning, calling it "folly" that threatened to undermine rather than cement free speech protections.

The District of Columbia and all but four states have some form of hate crime law, according to a brief filed in the case by the Anti-Defamation League of B'nai B'rith. Local officials expressed confidence yesterday that laws in the District, Maryland and Virginia would not be affected by yesterday's ruling, but First Amendment lawyers said they were far less optimistic.

"I think it makes almost all of them unconstitutional," said College of William and Mary law professor Rodney A. Smolla, a free speech expert who has written on speech codes. "The court went out of its way to enact a barrier against content-based regulation of speech that has broad implications for all of First Amendment law and goes well beyond the immediate problem it had before it."

Some other experts were not as strong in their views as Smolla, but agreed that the ruling at the very least cast doubt on the constitutionality of other laws and hate speech codes on public college campuses.

"We haven't crafted one that we think would pass muster [after yesterday's ruling] but we're not ready to reach the conclusion that none would," said Deanna Duby of People for the American Way, which argued in favor of the St. Paul law.

Debating Hate Speech and Free Speech

The case, *R.A.V. v. St. Paul*, comes at a time of national debate over hate speech laws and campus speech codes that many conservatives and some liberals see as imposing a regime of "political correctness."

With the desire to punish racist intimidation colliding with free speech concerns, the case split groups that are normally allied. Some organizations—the Anti-Defamation League, the NAACP [National Association for the Advancement of Colored People] and People for the American Way—supported the law's constitutionality; others, including the American Civil Liberties Union and the American Jewish Congress, argued against it.

The case had its start in the early morning hours of June 21, 1990, when Russ and Laura Jones, a black family who had recently moved onto an all-white block of east St. Paul, awoke to see a crudely made cross burning in their yard.

Robert Viktora, then 17, was charged with violating a city ordinance similar to those adopted by many localities in recent years in an effort to combat prejudice. It prohibited the display of offensive graffiti or symbols likely to arouse "anger, alarm or resentment in others on the basis of race, color, creed, religion or gender," and specifically cited the Nazi swastika and burning cross.

Penalizing Hate Speech Content Unconstitutional

The Minnesota Supreme Court upheld the law, saying it applied only to speech that was so incendiary as to constitute "fighting words"—conduct that "itself inflicts injury or tends to incite immediate violence." The high court, in earlier cases, has said such "fighting words"—like speech that is obscene or libelous—do not merit protection under the First Amendment.

But Scalia said that even within the category of "fighting words," the government cannot penalize some words and omit others based on their content. "The government," he said, "may not regulate use based on hostility—or favoritism—towards the underlying message expressed."

The problem with the St. Paul ordinance, he said, is that "displays containing abusive invective, no matter how vicious or severe, are permissible unless they are addressed to one of the specified disfavored topics. Those who wish to use 'fighting words' in connection with other ideas—to express hostility, for example, on the basis of political affiliation, union membership, or homosexuality—are not covered. The First Amendment does not permit St. Paul to impose special prohibitions on those speakers who express views on disfavored subjects."

Although the city might want to send a message to citizens that racial and religious intolerance is bad and display its "special hostility towards the particular biases thus singled out," Scalia said, "that is precisely what the First Amendment forbids. The politicians of St. Paul are entitled to express that hostility—but not through the means of imposing unique limitations upon speakers who (however benightedly) disagree."

He added: "Let there be no mistake about our belief that burning a cross in someone's front yard is reprehensible. But

St. Paul has sufficient means at its disposal to prevent such behavior without adding the First Amendment to the fire."

He said the youth could be prosecuted for arson, criminal damage to property and other crimes.

Chief Justice William H. Rehnquist and Justices Anthony M. Kennedy, David H. Souter and Clarence Thomas joined the opinion.

Concurring Dissent

The concurring justices, in opinions that sounded far more like dissents, accused the majority of going out of its way to rewrite First Amendment law.

In an opinion by White, they said the ordinance could easily have been found invalid under the court's "fighting words" precedents, on the ground that it was "fatally overbroad because it criminalizes not only unprotected expression but expression protected by the First Amendment."

White warned that the majority approach turned on its head the general "strict scrutiny" method of judging free speech cases: that restrictions on expression must be supported by a compelling interest (in this case, all justices agreed that protecting members of historically disadvantaged groups sufficed) and be as narrowly written as possible. Instead of narrow bans on speech, White said, the majority view would result in broader prohibitions.

"Under the majority's view, a narrowly drawn, content-based ordinance could never pass constitutional muster if the object of that legislation could be accomplished by banning a wider category of speech. This appears to be a general renunciation of strict scrutiny review, a fundamental tool of First Amendment analysis."

In a separate concurrence, Blackmun said the majority "manipulated doctrine to strike down an ordinance whose premise it opposed, namely that racial threats and verbal assaults are of greater harm than other fighting words." Blackmun added, "I fear that the court has been distracted from its proper mission by the temptation to decide the issue over 'politically correct speech' and 'cultural diversity,' neither of which is presented here."

"I see no First Amendment values that are compromised by a law that prohibits hoodlums from driving minorities out of their homes by burning crosses on their lawns," Blackmun said, "but I see great harm in preventing the people of St. Paul from specifically punishing the race-based fighting words that so prejudice their community."

Stevens also looked outside the courtroom to the streets of Los Angeles in arguing that the court erred in tying officials' hands to punish hate speech. "One need look no further than the recent social unrest in the nation's cities to see that race-based threats may cause more harm to society and to individuals than other threats," he said.

"Although it is regrettable that race occupies such a place and is so incendiary an issue, until the nation matures beyond that condition, laws such as St. Paul's ordinance will remain reasonable and justifiable."

Questioning the Validity of Other Hate Crime Laws

Michael Lieberman of the Anti-Defamation League and Jack Tunheim, chief deputy attorney general in Minnesota, expressed optimism that laws providing enhanced penalties for bias-related crimes will survive under the new test. The court yesterday did not specifically address such laws.

In those situations, Tunheim said, "the conduct involved is already a crime. There is an additional element of bias toward a particular person for whatever reason that is not, at least in my view, the kind of speech-related regulation that is clearly implicated in the ordinance."

But Marc Stern of the American Jewish Congress said that the penalty-enhancement statutes are "very doubtful after today. . . . If you enhance for race and not for sexual orientation, you have the same content basis you have here" that invalidated the St. Paul ordinance.

"I think what it means is that statutes of that sort are going to have to be written in content-neutral terms," said Steven Shapiro of the American Civil Liberties Union.

"A law that says you can't deface property is clearly okay. A law that says you can't deface property by painting swastikas but not any other kind of defacement is probably unconstitutional. . . . The only thing you can say for sure is that people are going to be suing over this stuff."

> *"In* R.A.V. v. City of St. Paul, *the Court held a hate crime ordinance unconstitutional under the First Amendment."*

Hate Crime Laws Prove Difficult to Legislate

Michael S. Degan

In the following viewpoint, Michael S. Degan defines hate crimes as heinous criminal acts directed against a victim due to his or her affiliation with a particular group, such as race, religion, or sexual orientation. Degan points to evidence showing an increase in race-based violence as the impetus for legislation that restricts hate crimes. However, he adds, such legislation presents freedom of speech questions. The writer reports that the first Supreme Court test of hate crime statutes came in R.A.V. v. City of St. Paul *(1992), in which the offenders burned a cross inside the fenced yard of an African American family. The issue before the Court was whether the city ordinance prohibiting disorderly conduct directed against a member of a minority group violated the free speech guarantee of the First Amendment. Although the Justices disagreed on the reasoning, they agreed unanimously that the city law restricted the protected right of free speech in the Constitution.*

In 1993, Michael S. Degan was a member of the Law Review *and a student at Creighton University School of Law.*

Hate crimes are criminal acts committed against particular victims because of the assailants' perceptions of the victims' race, national origin, religion, or other bias-related

Michael S. Degan, "Adding the First Amendment to the Fire: Cross Burning and Hate Crime Laws," *Creighton Law Review*, vol. 26, June 1993, pp. 1109–1120.

classification. Such acts add a particularly heinous component to conduct already classified as criminal because they are inflicted on the victims solely because of the assailants' hatred of the particular class to which the victim belongs. The beating of motorist Rodney King, the beating of truck driver Reginald Denny, and the violence in Los Angeles, California, during the spring of 1992, vividly displayed both the abhorrent nature of hate crimes and their incendiary tendency to ignite further violence.

Recent statistical evidence has shown an alarming increase in racially motivated violence. Most states have responded with legislation designed to curtail hate crimes. These laws have employed a variety of techniques designed to discourage bias-motivated behavior, such as creating separate criminal classifications for hate crimes and increasing the penalties for existing crimes when a bias-related motivation is found.

Raising Free Speech Issues

Although legislatures may unquestionably prohibit acts of violence, legislative attempts to specifically punish bias-motivated conduct raise serious First Amendment questions. The First Amendment guarantees one of our most cherished and fundamental rights—the right to voice one's views without fear of governmental reprisal. As the United States Supreme Court has stated, "If there is a bedrock principle underlying the First Amendment, it is that the government may not prohibit the expression of an idea simply because society finds the idea itself offensive or disagreeable." No matter how offensive a person's viewpoint may be, the fundamental axiom remains that the Constitution protects both thought and expression. As the Supreme Court has stated, "At the heart of the First Amendment is the notion that an individual should be free to believe as he will, and that in a free society one's beliefs should be shaped by his mind and his conscience rather than coerced by the State."

Yet the Supreme Court has historically viewed the First Amendment as subject to certain well-defined limits. The Court has held that First Amendment protection does not extend to certain types of speech that contain "no essential part of any exposition of ideas." Expression amounting to fighting words, private libel, and obscenity are examples of speech traditionally considered to be entirely outside the scope of First Amendment protection. Within these categories of unprotected speech, governments have generally been given a free hand to restrict speech. Additionally, the Supreme Court has recognized circumstances in which governments may constitutionally regulate protected speech. For example, governments may constitutionally prohibit individuals from yelling "fire" in crowded movie theaters.

Until recently, however, the Court had never ruled on the constitutionality of legislation designed to curb hate crimes. In *R.A.V. v. City of St. Paul*, the Court held a hate crime ordinance unconstitutional under the First Amendment. But the Court's opinion is problematic. The rule the Court set forth in *R.A.V.* is unwieldy, the exceptions to the general rule articulated by the Court are unclear, and the decision fails to provide guidance for lawmakers and lower courts attempting to determine the constitutionality of hate crime laws. . . .

Defining Hate Crime and Hate Speech

"Hate crime" has been broadly defined as the intentional selection of a victim in the commission of a criminal act based on an assailant's perception of the victim as belonging to a particular class. Generally, victims of hate crimes are selected based on their race, national origin, religion, sexual orientation, or creed. Thus, the beating of a Latino youth because of the aggressor's perception that the victim belongs to a particular disfavored group constitutes a hate crime.

In contrast, "hate speech" refers to language containing a negative connotation uttered in a derogatory fashion because of a victim's race, national origin, religion, sex, creed, or membership (real or perceived) in any other group or class. Thus, epithets such as "nigger," "wetback," "honkey," "kike," "gook," "spic," "faggot," "wop," or "mick," constitute hate speech when addressed to persons perceived to be members of the disfavored class. Whereas hate crimes involve the bias-related selection of a victim in the commission of an otherwise criminal act, hate speech refers only to the biased content of certain speech.

Theoretically, hate crimes do not necessarily contain an element of speech because an individual could remain silent during the commission of a hate crime, but the surrounding circumstances nevertheless may reveal a biased motive. However, a determination that an assailant has committed a hate crime generally requires the presence of spoken words reflecting the assailant's biased motive. Thus, a practical definition of hate crime would contain three elements: (1) a criminal act, (2) committed against a victim because of the victim's membership in a particular class, and (3) usually accompanied by bias-related speech.

Restricting Hate Crimes and Hate Speech

Hate crimes and hate speech are especially problematic because of the abhorrent effects they have on the victims. Recent studies have shown that victims of hate messages suffer emotional and physiological problems, including high blood pressure, sleep disorders, post-traumatic stress disorders, hypertension, and various forms of psychosis. Prolonged exposure to hate attacks perpetuates feelings of inferiority and helplessness among members of historically persecuted classes. These feelings often result in subconscious behavior modification by minorities to avoid further exposure to hate messages. Minorities therefore are prevented from fully assimilating into society because such hate messages often force minority members to change jobs, relocate, or forgo educational opportunities. Because of the invidious nature of hate crimes and hate speech, several commentators have called for legislative responses to hate crime.

Other writers, although recognizing the serious nature of the problems that hate crime and hate speech create for the victims, have argued that allowing lawmakers to restrict hate crime and hate speech would impermissibly encroach on the guarantees of the First Amendment. One commentator has noted that the regulation of hate crimes is complicated by the presence of two "slippery slopes." First, the removal of hate speech from First Amendment protection will allow for the imposition of restrictions on other forms of "offensive" speech. The same arguments advanced in favor of restricting racist hate speech could be advanced in support of bans on derogatory remarks directed at women, homosexuals, obese individuals, the disabled, the elderly, or any other class or group subjected to discrimination because of a physical trait or characteristic.

The second difficulty arises in attempting to delimit what language or expression is sufficiently "offensive" to constitute hate speech. Beyond the typical varieties of hate speech are words that could be used in a demeaning and derogatory fashion, despite their facial benevolence. Certain racial epithets may be given a hostile or benevolent meaning depending on the context, as demonstrated by the frequent use of the term "nigger" between some African Americans not as an insult, but as a term of endearment.

The questions that arise when attempting to define "hate crime" and "hate speech" demonstrate the essence of the problem presented by hate crime legislation. Because lawmakers are unable to make principled distinctions between what is and what is not "hate crime," any attempt to demarcate the boundaries of hate crime legislation becomes an arbitrary exercise. For example, should the definitions of hate crime and hate speech be limited to only racist speech and violence?

Should gay-bashing or sexist speech and violence be included within the scope of hate crime and hate speech laws? What language and conduct are sufficient to fall within these categories once the broader classes of biased speech and conduct are defined? These questions are central to the hate crime and hate speech issues.

Legislating Responses

Several states have responded to recent increases in bias-motivated violence by enacting legislation designed to punish such activity. Lawmakers have generally employed two types of criminal restrictions. The first type of hate crime law increases the penalty for a crime motivated by hatred. These "penalty enhancement" laws increase the penalty associated with the underlying criminal act, such as assault, trespass, or battery, where a biased motivation is found. The second type of hate crime statute treats hate crime as a separate substantive crime.

Most states that have enacted penalty enhancement hate crime laws have adopted the language of the model hate crime statute drafted by the Anti-Defamation League (ADL). The ADL model statute provides:

> A. A person commits the crime of intimidation if, by reason of the actual or perceived race, color, religion, national origin or sexual orientation of another individual or group of individuals, he violates the code provision for criminal trespass, criminal mischief, harassment, menacing, assault and/or any other appropriate statutorily proscribed criminal conduct.
>
> B. Intimidation is a misdemeanor/felony the degree of criminal liability should be made contingent upon the severity of the injury incited or the property lost or damaged. Other states have drafted their own penalty enhancement hate crime laws loosely based on the ADL concept.

The other type of hate crime law creates a separate substantive criminal category for bias-motivated activity which may be punished regardless of whether the underlying conduct is a punishable offense. One example of this type of law penalizes any individual who knowingly places on private or public property any symbol or characterization known to be offensive to members of a particular race, creed, color, religion, or gender. For example, an individual may violate such a law by burning a cross in front of the residence of an African American, regardless of whether the assailant has violated any other law.

R.A.V. v. City of St. Paul

The United States Supreme Court addressed the constitutionality of a hate crime law in *R.A.V. v. City of St. Paul.* In the early morning hours of June 21, 1990, Robert A. Viktora and several accomplices erected and burned a cross inside the fenced yard of an African American family living in a residential neighborhood. Viktora was arrested and charged under the St. Paul Bias-Motivated Crime Ordinance which provided:

> Whoever places on public or private property a symbol, object, appellation, characterization or graffiti, included but not limited to, a burning cross or Nazi swastika, which one knows or has reasonable grounds to know arouses anger, alarm, or resentment in others on the basis of race, color, creed, religion, or gender commits disorderly conduct and shall be guilty of a misdemeanor.

Although Viktora's conduct could have been punished under several other ordinances that carried stiffer penalties, including prohibitions of terroristic threats, arson, or destruction of property, the prosecution chose to charge Viktora under the St. Paul Bias-Motivated Crime Ordinance. . . .

Although the Court was unanimous in holding that the St. Paul ordinance was invalid under the First Amendment, the members of the Court disagreed in the reasoning supporting the judgment.

Analyzing *R.A.V.*

Justice Antonin Scalia, writing for the Court, adopted the Minnesota Supreme Court narrowing construction, which limited the reach of the ordinance to fighting words. The Court nevertheless ruled that the ordinance was facially invalid. The Court began its analysis with the proposition that all content-based restrictions of speech are presumptively invalid.

The Court noted, however, that it has allowed content-based restrictions of a few categories of traditionally unprotected speech, such as fighting words, private libel, and obscenity. Yet the Court stated that these categories of speech are not entirely without First Amendment protection:

> These categories of speech can, consistently with the First Amendment, be regulated because of their constitutionally proscribable content (obscenity, defamation, etc.)—not that they are categories of speech entirely invisible to the Constitution, so that they may be made the vehicles for content discrimination unrelated to their distinctively proscribable content.

The Court articulated a constitutionally significant distinction between proscribable and nonproscribable elements of traditionally unprotected speech. To illustrate this point, the Court reasoned that governments may constitutionally restrict libel because libelous statements themselves constitute proscribable elements of speech. However, governments may not restrict only libel critical of the government because the political element of such statements constitutes a nonproscribable element of speech. Thus, the presence of a traditionally proscribable element does not deprive speech of all constitutional protection.

The Court noted that its previous decisions had stood for the proposition that when restricting expressive conduct, governments may freely regulate the underlying proscribable conduct because of the action involved, but not because of the content of the message conveyed. Similarly, governments may place reasonable limits on the time, place, and manner of speech, as long as the restrictions are unrelated to the content of the messages. Thus, for example, governments may validly regulate trucks equipped with public address speakers ("sound trucks") with reasonable time, place, and manner restrictions because a proscribable element, noise, is present. However, governments may not regulate sound trucks based on the content of the message being broadcast. In analogizing fighting words to a sound truck, the Court reasoned that "both can be used to convey an idea; but neither has, in and of itself, a claim upon the First Amendment. . . . However the government may not regulate speech based on hostility—or favoritism—towards the underlying message expressed." The Court concluded that all content-based restrictions of speech are presumptively invalid, including content-based restrictions of subclasses of traditionally unprotected speech.

"Some people's freedom hurts other people's equality."

The Supreme Court Erred in *R.A.V. v. City of St. Paul*

Andrea L. Crowley

When faced with whether a St. Paul ordinance prohibiting hate crime and hate speech was unconstitutional, the Supreme Court ruled the city law was a disallowed content-based regulation of speech. In the following viewpoint, Andrea Crowley suggests that the Court failed to recognize the city's compelling interest in enacting a law that protected minority groups, promoted tolerance of groups traditionally subject to discrimination, and curbed the use of hate crimes to incite feelings of inequality and insecurity. She also concludes that the Court decision was inconsistent with other First Amendment Court rulings that allow laws against immorality, such as nude dancing and child pornography. She maintains that hate speech, like child pornography, can cause long-lasting emotional effects on children; hence, ordinances prohibiting hate speech and hate crimes should be permitted. Crowley reasons that in failing to uphold the city hate speech statute, the Court gives hate crime offenders a "green light." This article was written while Andrea L. Crowley was a law student at Boston College Law School. She is currently a practicing attorney in Boston.

In 1992, in *R.A.V. v. City of St. Paul*, the United States Supreme Court was faced with the question of whether the St. Paul, Minnesota, Bias-Motivated Crime Ordinance violated

Andrea L. Crowley, "*R.A.V. v. City of St. Paul*: How the Supreme Court Missed the Writing on the Wall," *Boston College Law Review*, July 1993. Reproduced by permission.

the First Amendment. As in the case of *Chaplinsky* [*Chaplinsky v. New Hampshire*, 1942], *Roth* [*Roth v. United States*, 1957], *Ferber* [*New York v. Ferber*, 1982], and *Barnes* [*Barnes v. Glen Theatre*, 1991], the Supreme Court had to decide whether it would fashion an exception to First Amendment protection. The Court refused to allow St. Paul to regulate hate speech through its ordinance, holding that the Bias-Motivated Crime Ordinance was unconstitutional. The majority based its holding on their assertion that the St. Paul Bias-Motivated Crime Ordinance was an impermissible content-based regulation of speech. The concurring Justices, three of whom wrote separately, agreed that the ordinance was unconstitutional, but based their opinions on a finding of overbreadth.

R.A.V., a minor, was charged under the St. Paul Bias-Motivated Crime Ordinance for burning a cross in the yard of an African American family's home. The ordinance made it a misdemeanor to place a symbol on public or private property that one knows arouses anger, alarm or resentment on the basis of race, color, creed, religion or gender. . . .

Hate Speech as an Unprotected Category of Speech

Some people's freedom hurts other people's equality.

In striking down St. Paul's Bias-Motivated Crime Ordinance, the Supreme Court abandoned long accepted First Amendment doctrine to avoid opening the door for a more narrowly drawn ordinance to be considered constitutional. The Court's categorical refusal to allow states to restrict biased speech, especially when the restriction applies to biased fighting words, contravenes traditional notions of First Amendment law. Further, the *R.A.V.* decision ignores the conclusions of forty-six states that there is a compelling state interest in displaying the majorities' viewpoint that racial, ethnic, religious and gender-based fighting words will not be tolerated, and in ensuring that a huge segment of America's population is protected from the indignities and the physiological and psychological effects of bias-motivated speech. Finally, the Court's language and its treatment of the St. Paul ordinance is totally contradictory to the Court's own treatment of other areas of restricted speech because of its insensitivity to minorities and the psychological damage incurred as a result of hate crimes.

The majority distorted traditional First Amendment jurisprudence in *R.A.V.* Rather than applying strict scrutiny to the ordinance to determine if a compelling state interest existed for the regulation of bias-motivated fighting words, the majority decided that fighting words, words that fall outside the First Amendment, deserve constitutional protection. This proposition seems contrary to logic and precedent: *Chaplinsky* held that fighting words are of so little value that they do not deserve constitutional protection. Under *R.A.V.*, however, bias-motivated fighting words, a subset of a category of unprotected speech, can arguably receive more protection than neutral fighting words. The majority's refusal to allow St. Paul to punish bias-motivated fighting words contravenes First Amendment analysis as it was developed in *Chaplinsky, Roth, Barnes* and *Ferber* because St. Paul articulated a compelling state interest, the Court has recognized that certain speech has little value, and the preservation of morality in society can justify an infringement on certain speech.

A Compelling State Interest

Assuming that the St. Paul ordinance is a content-based regulation of fighting words, it must serve a compelling state interest to be considered constitutional. In refusing to accept St. Paul's asserted interests in regulating bias-motivated fighting words, the Court ignored its own precedents and revealed its lack of concern for the victims of hate speech. Although the Court allegedly accepted that St. Paul had an interest in promoting tolerance and protecting minority groups that have been historically subject to discrimination, it suggested that St. Paul could achieve the same goals by enacting a statute that proscribed all fighting words. A neutral fighting words statute, however, would not serve St. Paul's articulated interest because it would not target the most damaging aspect of bias-motivated fighting words—their message of racial hatred. The Court's assertion that a neutral statute would serve St. Paul's interests reveals that it does find racially prejudiced speech and conduct morally culpable.

A community such as St. Paul has an interest in directly facing the issues of racial, ethnic, religious and gender inequality and combating the dangers of supremacist attacks on individuals based on their membership in a certain group. . . . Messages of inequality serve to imprint on their minority listeners a belief in their own inequality and lack of self-worth. An individual who sees him- or herself as less important or less valued in society will contribute less to society. More importantly, the evidence that black children suffer from low self-esteem and often carry this feeling into adulthood resulting in more severe symptoms such as alcoholism, drug addiction or unemployment reinforces the need for communities to take a strong stance against racial bias. St. Paul, and society as a whole, have a compelling interest in curbing the use of bias-motivated crimes as a tool for securing the social inequality of certain groups, and in voicing its intolerance for actions and words that contribute to negative characteristics in targeted groups.

The United States Supreme Court, as recently as 1991, has held that communities can prohibit some types of expression in order to protect or promote a certain moral climate. In refusing to apply this reasoning to the St. Paul ordinance, the Court has implicitly decided that racist fighting words are morally acceptable in St. Paul and the rest of the United States. The Court has also explicitly revealed its willingness to allow regulation in areas where they find the activity in controversy morally culpable, but not in the areas where they refuse to recognize the immoral nature of the activity.

For example, in *Barnes*, a case decided one year before *R.A.V.*, the Court upheld Indiana's prohibition on nude dancing on the basis of preserving morality. In *Barnes*, Justice [Antonin] Scalia championed the promotion of morals as the basis for state regulation of certain speech. The same argument exists with hate speech. *Webster's Dictionary of Modern English* defines immoral as "corrupt" or "unethical." Society has long recognized that messages of racial, ethnic, religious and gender-based supremacy are corrupt messages and ones that are contradictory to the guarantees of equality and justice for all. The Court had ample opportunity to uphold the St. Paul ordinance as an expression of St. Paul's belief in the morality of equality. In fact, when compared to the prohibition in *Barnes*, involving a statute regulating public nudity, the St. Paul ordinance is even more essential for protecting the moral fabric of our society. Nudity and nude dancing are essentially victimless activities engaged in by consenting adults. On the other hand, there are real victims who suffer from crimes motivated by racial bias.

Victims of Hate Speech

The compelling interest in regulating hate speech, and the argument for its regulation as an expression against the immorality of hate speech, can most likely find acceptance if viewed in light of the victims of hate crimes. Child pornography is an area of regulated speech that has received this type of analysis. In *Ferber*, the Court examined the damage to children involved in child pornography. The Court cited the negative effects on children who participate in child pornography, including their probable sexual abuse and exploitation, the inability to develop healthy adult relationships later in life, sexual dysfunctions and the tendency to become sexual abusers. In accepting the possible avoidance of these conditions as a compelling state interest that justified the prohibition of child pornography, the Court asserted that the interest in protecting the physical and psychological health and welfare of children is "beyond the need for elaboration." After all, a society that does not value the psychological well-being of its children does not value the well-being of its own future.

A similar argument can be made for the regulation of hate crimes. Hate crimes are known to cause physical and emotional illness in victims. In addition to causing fear and anger, hate speech perpetuates historical stereotypes that have tangible negative effects on its victims. Like children who participate in child pornography, the victims of hate crimes suffer the long-lasting effects of racial, ethnic, religious and gender bias. Child pornography statistics revealed the danger to children inherent in the industry and were used to support what most people already believed—child pornography is dangerous and of little social value. Similarly, the data set out in section I of this Note supports what psychologists and forty-six states already know—bias-motivated crimes are the ultimate form of racial prejudice and are not only immoral but result in lowered self-esteem, a sense of worthlessness, lack of motivation for success or contribution to society, and in some cases, severe emotional and physical distress in their victims.

The Court should have fashioned the same argument against hate speech that it invoked against child pornography. The speech in question, bias-motivated fighting words, is of so little value that the dangerous and lasting effects of hate speech outweigh any value they might bring to society. In the case of child pornography, the fact that most people considered child pornography to be essentially devoid of artistic, social or political value, in conjunction with the overwhelming evidence that it had serious effects on the children involved in its making, allowed the Court to uphold a content-based regulation. The same reasoning would apply in the case of bias-motivated fighting words (the words targeted by the St. Paul ordinance):

fighting words are not considered speech for purposes of the First Amendment, therefore in conjunction with the evidence that there are substantial negative effects of racially motivated speech on targeted groups, the Court could have upheld the St. Paul ordinance.

Critics may argue that the interest in regulating child pornography stems from the damage done specifically to children. Although racist hate speech may often be targeted at adults, the overall societal prejudice conveyed transcends generations and perpetuates negative stereotypes. By not allowing the regulation of racist fighting words, the United States Supreme Court allows for the damaging effects of prejudice to be passed on to future generations. Thus, as in the case of child pornography, there are innocent victims at stake. . . .

The Court's treatment of hate crime legislation in *R.A.V. v. St. Paul* signals a dangerous green light for those who want to intimidate and threaten members of racial, ethnic, religious and gender groups. The Court abandoned traditional First Amendment doctrine and virtually abolished any hope that states can effectively regulate criminal activity based on notions of supremacy. The Court can, however, abandon this interpretation and accept that states have a compelling interest in rejecting criminal messages of inequality based on common notions of morality and the need to safeguard certain individuals and minority groups from the lasting effects of hate speech. By recognizing the damage that hate speech inflicts on its victims, the Court can appreciate the need for ordinances like the St. Paul Bias-Motivated Crime Ordinance and find ample precedent for deeming them constitutional.

Chapter 2

Allowing Sentencing Enhancements for Hate Crimes

Case Overview

Wisconsin v. Mitchell (1993)

In a landmark case, the Supreme Court upheld the constitutionality of laws that provide increased punishment for hate crimes. Chief Justice William Rehnquist, in *Wisconsin v. Mitchell*, declared that penalty enhancement laws do not violate either the First Amendment's guarantee of freedom of speech or the Fourteenth Amendment's Equal Protection Clause.

The crime in question involved a group of young black men and boys who had gathered in an apartment in Kenosha, Wisconsin, in 1989. Several people in the group discussed the movie *Mississippi Burning*, particularly a scene in which a white man beat a black boy who was praying. When the group went outside, Mitchell incited their anger by asking: "Do you feel all hyped up to move on some white people?" Mitchell then pointed out a white boy walking by and said, "There goes a white boy; go get him." The group assaulted the boy and stole his tennis shoes. The boy was beaten so severely he remained in a coma for four days.

The state of Wisconsin charged Mitchell with aggravated battery and a jury found him guilty. Normally, such a crime carried maximum punishment of two years in prison. Wisconsin, however, had a penalty enhancement statute that increased the maximum penalty whenever an assailant picked his victim based on an individual's "race, religion, color, disability, sexual orientation, national origin, or ancestry." Under the penalty enhancement law, the court sentenced Mitchell to four years in prison. The defense argued the increased sentence punished people for their thoughts and beliefs, thus violating the First Amendment.

Nevertheless, Chief Justice Rehnquist ruled that the First Amendment was never intended to protect violence. He contended that hate crimes must be stopped. Since hate crimes can lead to further violence, emotional distress, and unrest in the community, states are permitted to discourage hate crimes by punishing them more harshly than other crimes. Thus, reasoned the Chief Justice, the Wisconsin law passed Constitutional muster. He also noted that judges traditionally are permitted to consider a wide variety of factors when rendering a defendant's sentence; therefore, the Constitution places no prohibition on evidence regarding a person's beliefs and associations. The Chief Justice also contrasted the ordinance in *R.A.V. v. City of St. Paul*, which was specifically directed at speech, with the Wisconsin statute, which was expressly directed at conduct. The Chief Justice also concluded that the Wisconsin law cannot be deemed overbroad as it presented no foreseeable "chilling effect" on free speech.

Although some commentators bemoaned an alleged weakening of First Amendment rights, the Supreme Court's decision was truly unanimous in that no other Justice offered any disagreement on the reasoning of the majority decision or raised any First Amendment objections regarding the rights of states to enact hate crime sentencing laws or to use evidence of motive in sentencing. Thus the ruling, which was supported by the other forty-nine states, was both decisive and powerful—ending the uncertainty that had existed since the holding from *R.A.V. v. City of St. Paul* the prior year.

"A physical assault is not by any stretch of the imagination expressive conduct protected by the First Amendment."

The Court's Decision: States May Enhance Sentences for Bias-Motivated Crime

William Rehnquist

In Wisconsin v. Mitchell, *a unanimous decision, William Rehnquist ruled that the First Amendment freedom of speech rights are not violated by hate crime penalty enhancement statutes. Noting that judges traditionally are permitted to consider a wide variety of factors when rendering a defendant's sentence, Rehnquist declares in the following majority opinion that the Constitution places no prohibition on evidence regarding a person's beliefs and associations. He distinguishes the ordinance in* R.A.V. v. City of St. Paul, *which was specifically directed at speech, from the Wisconsin statute which is explicitly directed at conduct. Moreover, Rehnquist indicates that Wisconsin sought to punish bias-inspired conduct—behavior that inflicts not only individual injury, but also societal harm. William H. Rehnquist was appointed to the Supreme Court in 1972 as an associate justice by President Richard Nixon. In 1986 he was elevated to Chief Justice by President Ronald Reagan, serving eighteen years as Chief Justice. He served on the Court until his retirement in 2005, the year in which he died from thyroid cancer.*

William Rehnquist, majority opinion, *Wisconsin v. Mitchell*, U.S. Supreme Court, 508 U.S. 47, in Legal Information Institute, Cornell University Law School, 1993.

On the evening of October 7, 1989, a group of young black men and boys, including Todd Mitchell, gathered at an apartment complex in Kenosha, Wisconsin. Several members of the group discussed a scene from the motion picture *Mississippi Burning*, in which a white man beat a young black boy who was praying. The group moved outside and Mitchell asked them: "'Do you all feel hyped up to move on some white people?'" Shortly thereafter, a young white boy approached the group on the opposite side of the street where they were standing. As the boy walked by, Mitchell said: "'You all want to f--- somebody up? There goes a white boy; go get him.'" Mitchell counted to three and pointed in the boy's direction. The group ran towards the boy, beat him severely, and stole his tennis shoes. The boy was rendered unconscious and remained in a coma for four days. . . .

After a jury trial in the Circuit Court for Kenosha County, Mitchell was convicted of aggravated battery. That offense ordinarily carries a maximum sentence of two years' imprisonment. But because the jury found that Mitchell had intentionally selected his victim because of the boy's race, the maximum sentence for Mitchell's offense was increased to seven years under § 939.645. That provision enhances the maximum penalty for an offense whenever the defendant "[i]ntentionally selects the person against whom the crime . . . is commited . . . because of the race, religion, color, disability, sexual orientation, national origin or ancestry of that person. . . ." The Circuit Court sentenced Mitchell to four years' imprisonment for the aggravated battery.

Mitchell unsuccessfully sought postconviction relief in the Circuit Court. Then he appealed his conviction and sentence, challenging the constitutionality of Wisconsin's penalty enhancement provision on First Amendment grounds. The Wisconsin Court of Appeals rejected Mitchell's challenge, but the Wisconsin Supreme Court reversed. The Supreme Court held that the statute "violates the First Amendment directly by punishing what the legislature has deemed to be offensive thought." It rejected the State's contention "that the statute punishes only the 'conduct' of intentional selection of a victim." According to the court, "[t]he statute punishes the 'because of' aspect of the defendant's selection, the *reason* the defendant selected the victim, the *motive* behind the selection." And under *R.A.V. v. St. Paul*, 505 U.S. (1992), "the Wisconsin legislature cannot criminalize bigoted thought with which it disagrees."

Speech Versus Conduct

The State argues that the statute does not punish bigoted thought, as the Supreme Court of Wisconsin said, but instead punishes only conduct. While this argument is literally correct, it does not dispose of Mitchell's First Amendment challenge. To be sure, our cases reject the "view that an apparently limitless variety of conduct can be labeled 'speech' whenever the person engaging in the conduct intends thereby to express an idea" [*United States v. O'Brien*, 1968]. Thus, a physical assault is not by any stretch of the imagination expressive conduct protected by the First Amendment.

But the fact remains that under the Wisconsin statute the same criminal conduct may be more heavily punished if the victim is selected because of his race or other protected status than if no such motive obtained. Thus, although the statute punishes criminal conduct, it enhances the maximum penalty for conduct motivated by a discriminatory point of view more severely than the same conduct engaged in for some other reason or for no reason at all. Because the only reason for the enhancement is the defendant's discriminatory motive for selecting his victim, Mitchell argues (and the Wisconsin Supreme Court held) that the statute violates the First Amendment by punishing offenders' bigoted beliefs.

Sentencing Factors

Traditionally, sentencing judges have considered a wide variety of factors in addition to evidence bearing on guilt in determining what sentence to impose on a convicted defendant. The defendant's motive for committing the offense is one important factor [*Tison v. Arizona*, 1987]: "Deeply ingrained in our legal tradition is the idea that the more purposeful is the criminal conduct, the more serious is the offense, and, therefore, the more severely it ought to be punished." Thus, in many States the commission of a murder, or other capital offense, for pecuniary [monetary] gain is a separate aggravating circumstance under the capital sentencing statute.

But it is equally true that a defendant's abstract beliefs, however obnoxious to most people, may not be taken into consideration by a sentencing judge. In *Dawson v. Delaware* the State introduced evidence at a capital sentencing hearing that the defendant was a member of a white supremacist prison gang. Because "the evidence proved nothing more than [the defendant's] abstract beliefs," we held that its admission violated the defendant's First Amendment rights. In so holding, however, we emphasized that "the Constitution does not erect a *per se* barrier to the admission of evidence concerning one's beliefs and associations at sentencing simply because those beliefs and associations are protected by the First Amendment." Thus, in *Barclay v. Florida* (1983), we allowed the sentencing judge to take into account the defendant's racial animus towards his victim. The evidence in that case showed that the defendant's membership in the Black Liberation Army and desire to provoke a "race war" were related to the murder of a white man for which he was convicted. Because "the elements of racial hatred in [the] murder" were relevant to several aggravating factors, we held that the trial judge permissibly took this evidence into account in sentencing the defendant to death.

Mitchell suggests that *Dawson* and *Barclay* are inapposite because they did not involve application of a penalty enhancement provision. But in *Barclay* we held that it was permissible for the sentencing court to consider the defendant's racial animus in determining whether he should be sentenced to death, surely the most severe "enhancement" of all. And the fact that the Wisconsin Legislature has decided, as a general matter, that bias motivated offenses warrant greater maximum penalties across the board does not alter the result here. For the primary responsibility for fixing criminal penalties lies with the legislature.

Discriminatory Motive

Mitchell argues that the Wisconsin penalty enhancement statute is invalid because it punishes the defendant's discriminatory motive, or reason, for acting. But motive plays the same role under the Wisconsin statute as it does under federal and state antidiscrimination laws, which we have previously upheld against constitutional challenge.

Nothing in our decision last term in *R.A.V.* compels a different result here. That case involved a First Amendment challenge to a municipal ordinance prohibiting the use of "'fighting words' that insult, or provoke violence, 'on the basis of race, color, creed, religion or gender'" (quoting St. Paul Bias-Motivated Crime Ordinance, St. Paul, Minn., Legis. Code § 292.02 (1990)). But whereas the ordinance struck down in *R.A.V.* was explicitly directed at expression, the statute in this case is aimed at conduct unprotected by the First Amendment.

Moreover, the Wisconsin statute singles out for enhancement bias inspired conduct because this conduct is thought to inflict greater individual and societal harm. For example, according to the State and its *amici* [a party not directly involved in the case, but who is allowed by the court to advise it on a point of law or some other aspect affecting the case], bias motivated crimes are more likely to provoke retaliatory crimes, inflict distinct emotional harms on their victims, and incite community unrest. The State's desire to redress these perceived harms provides an adequate explanation for its penalty enhancement provision over and above mere disagreement with offenders' beliefs or biases.

Effect on Free Speech

Finally, there remains to be considered Mitchell's argument that the Wisconsin statute is unconstitutionally overbroad because of its "chilling effect" on free speech. Mitchell argues (and the Wisconsin Supreme Court agreed) that the statute is "overbroad" because evidence of the defendant's prior speech or associations may be used to prove that the defendant intentionally selected his victim on account of the victim's protected status. Consequently, the argument goes, the statute impermissibly chills free expression with respect to such matters by those concerned about the possibility of enhanced sentences if they should in the future commit a criminal offense covered by the statute. We find no merit in this contention.

The sort of chill envisioned here is far more attenuated and unlikely than that contemplated in traditional "overbreadth" cases. We must conjure up a vision of a Wisconsin citizen suppressing his unpopular bigoted opinions for fear that if he later commits an offense covered by the statute, these opinions will be offered at trial to establish that he selected his victim on account of the victim's protected status, thus qualifying him for penalty enhancement. To stay within the realm of rationality, we must surely put to one side minor misdemeanor offenses covered by the statute, such as negligent operation of a motor vehicle for it is difficult, if not impossible, to conceive of a situation where such offenses would be racially motivated. We are left, then, with the prospect of a citizen suppressing his bigoted beliefs for fear that evidence of such beliefs will be introduced against him at trial if he commits a more serious offense against person or property. This is simply too speculative a hypothesis to support Mitchell's overbreadth claim.

Speech as Evidence of Intent

The First Amendment, moreover, does not prohibit the evidentiary use of speech to establish the elements of a crime or to prove motive or intent. Evidence of a defendant's previous declarations or statements is commonly admitted in criminal trials subject to evidentiary rules dealing with relevancy, reliability, and the like. Nearly half a century ago, in *Haupt v. United States* (1947), we rejected a contention similar to that advanced by Mitchell here. Haupt was tried for the offense of treason, which, as defined by the Constitution, may depend very much on proof of motive. To prove that the acts in question were committed out of "adherence to the enemy" rather than "parental solicitude," the Government introduced evidence of conversations that had taken place long prior to the indictment, some of which consisted of statements showing Haupt's sympathy with Germany and [Adolf] Hitler and hostility towards the United States. We rejected Haupt's argument that this evidence was improperly admitted. While "[s]uch testimony is to be scrutinized with care to be certain the statements are not expressions of mere lawful and permissible difference of opinion with our own government or quite proper appreciation of the land of birth," we held that "these statements . . . clearly were admissible on the question of intent and adherence to the enemy."

For the foregoing reasons, we hold that Mitchell's First Amendment rights were not violated by the application of the Wisconsin penalty enhancement provision in sentencing him. The judgment of the Supreme Court of Wisconsin is therefore reversed, and the case is remanded for further proceedings not inconsistent with this opinion.

> *"The Supreme Court's unanimity today barely reflected the lively and sometimes bitter debate around the country during the past few years over the hate-crime issue."*

Wisconsin v. Mitchell Empowers Hate Crime Laws

Linda Greenhouse

In this article, Linda Greenhouse suggests that in Wisconsin v. Mitchell *the Supreme Court has taken a "new approach" to penalizing crimes committed by offenders who choose their victims based on race, religion, or other personal traits. She notes that the decision supposed by a joint brief submitted by the forty-nine other states ended the uncertainty that had existed since the* R.A.V. v. City of St. Paul *holding from the year before where the court ruled a St. Paul ban on bias-motivated speech was unconstitutional. In upholding the Wisconsin statute that targeted hate crimes, Greenhouse concludes that the Court distinguished between unconstitutional laws directed at speech and laws directed at hate crime conduct; moreover the Court stressed the right to consider motive in the sentencing of bias-crime offenders.*

Linda Greenhouse is a reporter for The New York Times.

The Supreme Court gave its approval today to a new approach to punishing hate crimes, ruling unanimously that

Linda Greenhouse, "The Supreme Court: Hate Crimes; Justices Uphold Stiffer Sentences for Hate Crimes," *New York Times*, June 12, 1993.

states may impose harsher sentences on criminals who choose their victims on the basis of race, religion or other personal characteristics.

Chief Justice William H. Rehnquist's opinion for the Court upheld a Wisconsin state law that is similar to sentence-enhancement laws now on the books in more than half the states. In an unusual show of state unanimity, the 49 other states filed a joint brief in support of the Wisconsin law. With a similar Federal measure now under consideration in Congress, the [Bill] Clinton Administration also filed a brief in support of the Wisconsin law.

Succinctly and definitively, Chief Justice Rehnquist's opinion swept away the constitutional doubt that had surrounded the hate-crime issue for the past year. Last June [1992], the Court struck down a St. Paul ordinance that made certain expressions of racial and religious hatred into crimes.

Distinction Is Drawn

The opinion today drew a sharp distinction between the St. Paul ordinance and the much more common approach to hate crimes represented by the Wisconsin law. While the city ordinance the Court overturned last year was "explicitly directed at expression," Mr. Rehnquist said, "the statute in this case is aimed at conduct unprotected by the First Amendment."

Noting that judges have traditionally taken a convicted defendant's motive into account in deciding what sentence to impose, the Chief Justice said that legislatures could appropriately pass sentencing laws to reflect a judgment that crimes motivated by bias are more harmful than other crimes both to victims and to society at large.

The Wisconsin law is based on a model statute developed in the early 1980s by the Anti-Defamation League of B'nai B'rith, whose leaders hailed the decision today. Under this approach, the jury that has convicted a defendant of an existing crime—in this case, assault—then makes a separate judgment that the crime was motivated by bias and qualified for the increased sentence.

Defining Bias Crimes

The Wisconsin law defines as bias crimes those that are committed against a person or property "because of the race, religion, color, disability, sexual orientation, national origin or ancestry of that person or the owner or occupant of that property." Not all state laws include disability or sexual orientation.

The Supreme Court's unanimity today barely reflected the lively and sometimes bitter debate around the country during the past few years over the hate-crime issue. But divisions were apparent in the briefs filed with the Court. For example, while the American Civil Liberties Union supported the state law, that organization's Ohio affiliate filed a brief on the opposite side. The Ohio Supreme Court struck down a similar law last year, and the state's appeal from that ruling is before the Justices now.

Many traditionally liberal groups filed briefs supporting the Wisconsin law, including civil rights groups and organizations like People for the American Way. Many Jewish organizations supported the state. On the opposite side was the Center for Individual Rights, a Washington-based public interest law firm, which filed a brief describing the Wisconsin law as "expressly aimed at beliefs and perceptions, not conduct or speech."

Racial Incident in 1989

The challenge to the Wisconsin law was brought by a black man, Todd Mitchell, who was convicted in 1989 of leading an assault on a white teenager on a Kenosha street. "There goes a white boy; go get him," Mr. Mitchell told a group of young men and teenagers. The victim was in a coma for four days after the beating.

While the maximum penalty for aggravated battery, the crime for which Mr. Mitchell was convicted, is ordinarily two years in prison, the jury's separate finding that he had selected his victim because of race increased the possible sentence to seven years. The trial judge gave him a four-year sentence.

A state appeals court upheld the law, but the Wisconsin Supreme Court declared it unconstitutional last June, finding that the law had the effect of punishing thought. "The Wisconsin Legislature cannot criminalize bigoted thought with which it disagrees," the state court said.

The distinction between thought and expression on the one hand, and conduct on the other, thus became critical to the Justices' examination of the statute. During the argument in April, the Wisconsin Attorney General, James E. Doyle, was emphatic in describing his state's law as one aimed not at ideas but at a particular harmful form of criminal violence. The Justices appeared then to favor that approach.

Crossing the Line

In his opinion today, *Wisconsin v. Mitchell*, Chief Justice Rehnquist said that "a defendant's abstract beliefs, however obnoxious to most people, may not be taken into consideration by a sentencing judge." But he said that the belief is no longer abstract once it provides the motive for discriminatory action.

The Chief Justice noted that the Court had long upheld the constitutionality of the Federal Civil Rights Act of 1964, which prohibits employers from discriminating against an employee "because of such individual's race, color, religion, sex or national origin."

"Motive plays the same role under the Wisconsin statute" as under Federal and state anti-discrimination laws, he said.

Representative Charles E. Schumer, a Brooklyn Democrat who is sponsoring a Federal sentence-enhancement law for hate crimes, said today that the decision would help the progress of his legislation. The bill passed the House of Representatives last year [2002] but died in the Senate. It is now before the House Judiciary Committee.

Brian Levin, legal affairs director for the Center for the Study of Ethnic and Racial Violence, which is based in Edgewater, Colo., said today that hate crimes, while rarely detected or prosecuted today, were "very deterrable" if laws like the one the Court upheld today were used effectively by prosecutors and if the public was aware that the laws existed.

> *"The Court may have had the good intention of deterring views many consider reprehensible, but it did so at the expense of First Amendment rights."*

Wisconsin v. Mitchell Violates the First Amendment

Thomas D. Brooks

In the following viewpoint, Thomas Brooks concludes that the Supreme Court ruling in Wisconsin v. Mitchell *violates the First Amendment. In* Mitchell, *the Court held that the freedom of speech guarantee does not preclude a state from increasing the penalty for a crime if the defendant targeted the victim based on the victim's race, color, religion, disability, sexual orientation, national origin, or ancestry—as long as the enhanced penalty stems from violent conduct. Yet Brooks asserts that the Court relies on constitutionally protected hate speech to enhance the sentence. Therefore, he contends, the Court's decision reflects a retreat from* R.A.V. v. City of St. Paul *(1993); instead, the Court bases its ruling on cases that held that an offender's beliefs could be considered in sentencing. Though hate crimes are offensive to society, Brooks concludes that the right to free speech should not be trampled for purposes of sentencing. Thomas D. Brooks was a law student at Northwestern University in Chicago in 1994 when this essay was published.*

Thomas D. Brooks, "First Amendment - Penalty Enhancement for Hate Crimes: Content Regulation, Questionable State Interests and Non-Traditional Sentencing," *Journal of Criminal Law and Criminology*, vol. 84, Winter-Spring 1994, pp. 703–742.

[In *Wisconsin v. Mitchell*] the Supreme Court reversed the Wisconsin high court in a unanimous decision written by Chief Justice [William] Rehnquist. The Court's opinion addressed three issues. First, the Court considered its authority to question the Wisconsin high court's construction of the statute. Second, the Court explored whether the statute permissibly targeted nonexpressive conduct or impermissibly targeted expression. Finally, the Court looked at whether the statute was overbroad.

The Court dispatched the issue of statutory construction quickly. Although the Court is bound by a state supreme court's construction of the state's statute, the Court found that the Wisconsin high court had not actually construed the statute. The Court held that it was bound by a state supreme court's construction of a statute only when that construction consisted of "defining the meaning of a particular statutory word or phrase." Since the Wisconsin court looked only to the intent and effect of the statute and not to the meaning of its terms, the Supreme Court was not bound by the lower court's analysis and holding.

The Court next addressed the question of whether the statute targets expression. The state argued that the penalty-enhancement statute in [Todd] Mitchell's case punished the conduct of physical violence. The Court found that such conduct is not expressive.

This finding was not dispositive [decisive] however. The Court noted that, had Mitchell been convicted of a battery not tinged with bias, he could not have received the extra two years on his sentence. Thus, the Court found that Mitchell received the extra time on his sentence solely for his discriminatory motive.

Punishing Motive

Mitchell argued that imposing extra punishment for his motive violated his First Amendment rights. Mitchell contended

that punishing motive amounts to punishing thought and pointed to precedent holding that punishing thought is impermissible under the First Amendment. In particular, Mitchell argued that *R.A.V. v. City of St. Paul* stands for the proposition that even reprehensible, racist thought may not be singled out for punishment.

The Court rejected Mitchell's argument. The Court reasoned that the caveats against punishing thought do not apply to cases of criminal sentencing, of which the Court found Mitchell's an example. The Court found that, under statutory sentencing schemes, reprehensible motives often garner the offender a stiffer sentence. By way of example, the Court pointed out that murder for hire often receives a more severe penalty than does murder committed for more "mundane" reasons. Still, the Court emphasized that the defendant's motives or beliefs must be relevant to the crime at hand for them to be admissible during sentencing. . . .

The Court distinguished *Mitchell* from *R.A.V.* The Court reasoned that the statute at issue in *Mitchell* looks at motive in order to regulate non-expressive conduct, but the ordinance in *R.A.V.* simply regulated expression.

Harm and Extent of Hate Crimes

The greater harms inflicted by bias-motivated crimes also justify singling them out for punishment, the Court found. Crimes motivated by bias "are more likely to provoke retaliatory crimes, inflict distinct emotional harms on their victims, and incite community unrest."

The third issue addressed by the Court was that of overbreadth. The Court quickly dismissed Mitchell's argument that the Wisconsin statute is overly broad. The Court found implausible the contention that one already predisposed to expressing bigoted opinions would suppress those opinions for fear they would be brought up during a prosecution under the penalty-enhancement statute. The Court reasoned that the

nexus between the bigoted words and the possible subsequent prosecution was too loose. Moreover, the Court noted that the admissibility of evidence in criminal trials is governed by enough standards of relevancy and reliability to assuage worry in this scenario.

Decision Incorrect

Mitchell was incorrectly decided. The Court's holding hinges upon two questionable findings. First, the Court found that the Wisconsin penalty-enhancement statute in Mitchell's case punished the nonexpressive conduct of physical violence. This Note argues, however, that the statute did punish Mitchell's expression. If so, precedents ignored by the Court become controlling and lead to the conclusion that Wisconsin's approach violated the First Amendment. Second, the Court found Mitchell's case analogous to cases which—although they did not punish expression—did hold a criminal defendant's expressive activity admissible in procedures to determine the severity of sentence. *Mitchell*, however, is distinguishable from those cases on the grounds that Mitchell dealt with a penalty enhanced beyond the normal statutory range and the other cases did not.

Mitchell's conduct may be characterized in two ways as expression protected by the First Amendment. First, one can characterize him as having been engaged in speech, which is entitled to the greatest protection under the amendment. Although Mitchell's speech advocated violence and thus could have been regulated under the amendment, Wisconsin's regulation went too far in that it was not content-neutral. Alternatively, one can characterize Mitchell as having been engaged in expressive conduct, which is also protected, albeit to a lesser extent, under the First Amendment. Mitchell, it can be argued, was engaged in the expressive conduct of selecting a crime victim from one of certain, enumerated groups. Such conduct, contrary to the State's arguments, does not pose special dangers warranting state regulation. Moreover, Wisconsin's attempt to regulate this conduct directly and unnecessarily restricts free expression.

Regulating Speech and Conduct

A key holding of the Court—that the conduct at issue under the Wisconsin state was physical violence—is debatable. The Court accepted too easily the State's contention that the statute targets, and that Mitchell was engaged in, only nonexpressive conduct. Specifically, the Court characterized the statute's target and Mitchell's conduct as the "physical assault" of the victim. Two considerations weigh against this holding. First, Mitchell's conviction under the penalty enhancer appears to have resulted solely from his speech. In addition, First Amendment doctrine rejects criminal conviction based solely on the defendant's speech.

The prosecution must show two elements to secure a conviction under Wisconsin's penalty-enhancement statute. First, it must show that the defendant committed a predicate offense. Second, it must show that this offense was visited upon the victim because of the victim's membership in a certain group. The jury apparently convicted Mitchell of the predicate offense of aggravated battery as a party to the crime solely on the basis of his words. Mitchell maintained that he did not take part in the "physical assault," that he did not even cross to the victim's side of the street. Under section 939.05 of the Wisconsin statutes, "[w]hoever is concerned in the commission of a crime is a principal and may be charged with and convicted of the commission of the crime although he did not directly commit it." A person may be "concerned in the commission of the crime" if he "advises . . . another to commit it." Since Mitchell suggested that his comrades commit the battery upon Reddick, the jury could have found him guilty of aggravated battery as a party to the crime—the first element required under the penalty-enhancement statute—solely because of this advice.

Question of Evidence

Moreover, the only evidence available to establish the second element consisted of Mitchell's words. Since there was no other evidence offered of Mitchell's intent to commit a racial crime, his selection of a white person as the victim was evident only from what he said to his group. Thus, the fact that one element could have been proven solely by Mitchell's words and that the second element undeniably was proven solely by his words leads to the conclusion that Mitchell could have been convicted solely because of his words.

The First Amendment, however, forbids statutes from producing a criminal conviction solely on the basis of protected speech. . . .

The Courts holding in *Mitchell* remains questionable because it relies on two dubious conclusions. First, the Court held that Wisconsin's penalty-enhancement statute punished merely Mitchell's nonexpressive conduct of physical violence. This Note has argued that the statute actually punishes expression in contravention of First Amendment doctrine. The statute punishes speech and it punishes expressive conduct, according to this Note's analysis.

Second, the Court analogized Mitchell's case to others in which a criminal defendant's expression was held admissible in determining the severity of sentence. However, this Note has maintained that *Mitchell* can be distinguished from those cases. Those sentencing cases dealt with penalties within the normal statutory range for a given offense, but *Mitchell* involved sentencing beyond the usual statutory level for one offense.

The Court may have had the good intention of deterring views many consider reprehensible, but it did so at the expense of First Amendment rights.

"The existence of hate crime law dictates that illegal acts motivated by bias are inherently worse than the same acts done without such motivation."

Balancing Society's Rights and the Individual's Right of Free Speech

Joshua S. Geller

In this viewpoint, Joshua Geller discusses the practical and constitutional issues of Wisconsin v. Mitchell *regarding hate speech and declares that the Supreme Court ignored arguments that hate crime laws that punish violence do not violate the guarantee of freedom of speech. Thus, he reasons, the validation of hate crime laws indicates that conduct motivated by bias is by its nature worse than the same conduct without the evidence of hatred—especially since vulnerable victims are targeted. Another problem with hate crime laws, he asserts, is that the determination of motive is left to a jury, which may sympathize with either the victim or the offender. Geller concludes that by including motive in sentencing, hate crime statutes provide a balance between the societal benefits of sentence enhancement and the infringement of the offenders' speech rights. In 2005, Joshua S. Geller was a law student at Fordham University School of Law in New York City.*

Joshua S. Geller, "A Dangerous Mix: Mandatory Sentence Enhancements and the Use of Motive," *Fordham Urban Law Journal*, vol. 32, May 2005, pp. 623–647.

The Supreme Court ruled on the primary constitutional issues related to hate crime laws in *Wisconsin v. Mitchell.* In *Mitchell*, the Supreme Court overturned the decision of the Wisconsin Supreme Court, which had found that the state hate crime statute violated the First Amendment and was overbroad, leading to a chilling effect on speech. *Mitchell* involved a group of young black males who, after watching the film *Mississippi Burning*, became incensed and assaulted a white male as he was walking down the street. [Todd] Mitchell, the leader of the group, encouraged the assault and selected the victim because of his race. At the time, the maximum sentence in Wisconsin for aggravated battery was two years imprisonment, and this maximum was increased to seven years when the hate crime statute was applicable. Mitchell was sentenced to four years in prison.

The Supreme Court distinguished between the motives for committing a hate crime and the abstract beliefs of the defendant. Writing for the unanimous Court, Chief Justice [William] Rehnquist noted that while motive can be used as a factor in sentencing, the defendant's beliefs must not be taken into consideration when determining guilt. The opinion went on to discuss the harms posed to society by hate crimes, and concluded that "[t]he State's desire to redress these perceived harms provides an adequate explanation for its penalty-enhancement provision over and above mere disagreement with offenders' beliefs or biases."

Restrictions on Ideas and Beliefs

In effect, the Supreme Court made its decision by dismissing the constitutional arguments despite its insistence that the First Amendment does not place a per se barrier on the admission of evidence regarding the defendant's associations or beliefs. The problem, though, is not with the introduction of evidence regarding the defendant's beliefs, it is the use of those beliefs as evidence of the crime....

The result of this slight distinction is that a person could feel forced to engage in self-censorship for fear that an off-handed, off-color comment may one day be used against him in court if he is involved in an altercation with a member of the offended minority group.

Although the reduction of prejudice may be a goal of hate crime law, its restriction on thoughts and ideas because of a fear of imprisonment is problematic in both a practical and constitutional sense, and *Mitchell* does not resolve these concerns. People are allowed to express opinions; indeed the First Amendment protection of the freedom of speech is held sacrosanct. While the Supreme Court has stated numerous times that there are classes of speech that are not protected, unprotected speech may be prohibited by the government only when there is a basis for doing so.

The ability to prohibit speech in some contexts does not necessarily permit the blanket punishment of anyone who says it. The phrase "I hate Muslims," while repugnant, is not a crime; it may lead to a prison term, however, if made contemporaneously with the speaker's assault of a person of Middle Eastern descent and found by a jury to be the motivation for that attack. . . .

Moral Judgments of Hate Crime Offenses

The existence of hate crime law dictates that illegal acts motivated by bias are inherently worse than the same acts done without such motivation. The difference between a hate crime and a regular offense may be predicated on the inclusion of motive in the definition of the offense. This would suggest that the prosecution's assessment of motive should follow the same path as the already-existing inquiry into mens rea culpability [the criminal intent], in which purposeful behavior is more culpable than reckless behavior.

Motive differs from intent in that any number of different motivations can drive the commission of an act, a number of which are not clearly more or less "wrong" than any other. Therefore, while it is accepted as fair that the purposeful, premeditating murderer should be punished more severely than the reckless, accidental murderer, it is not axiomatic [self-evident] that the sadistic criminal is more or less blameworthy than the racially-biased one. Different types of motive do not have such stark distinctions and it is rather arbitrary to base the stringency of the punishment on one type over another.

The Vulnerability of Victims

It can also be argued that hate crime laws are justified because some members of society are more vulnerable to attack than others and therefore are deserving of more protection by the state under general equal protection principles. This theory would infer that vulnerability warrants determining the bias of the attacker. . . .

The problem with this theory is that any assault of another person is wrong. If the victim is a member of a racial minority, a religious minority, or has a certain sexual preference, the prosecution should not be led to the assumption that the reason for the assault was hatred of the victim's minority status, yet hate crime law seems to do just that. The approach of the vulnerability theory is simplistic in that even if an attack is not racially motivated, the punishment is still enhanced because of the victim's inherent vulnerability. The end result could then run contrary to the law's intent: for instance, if one Jew assaulted another, a prosecutor could jump to the conclusion that it was a hate crime, even if the attack had nothing to do with anti-Semitism. The defendant would then be faced with the prospect of an extended jail term, with only a jury's finding of motive providing a safety net.

To counter such arguments, it may be necessary to take the vulnerability theory even further. Hate crime laws can be justified specifically because of their use of motive; rather than being inflexible and punishing equally all assailants of minorities, by inquiring into motive the law punishes only those who act out of hate while still providing protection to vulnerable victims. The premise of this notion is that the victim of a hate-based crime has a protectable interest in the perpetrator's thoughts. By virtue of being selected as a target because of his identity, the hate crime victim is entitled to a greater interest in the defendant's motivation than would be available to the ordinary victim.

While an ordinary assault would not warrant such an intrusion, the extra wrong of selecting the victim because of bias provides the justification. These arguments force legislatures to pit the vulnerability of the victim against the difficulty of discerning the defendant's thoughts. The balance is delicate, and yet rather than safeguarding against bad decisions, statutory sentence enhancements function with the subtlety of a wrecking ball.

Jury Determination of Bias

The imprecision of determining motive is compounded by the danger inherent in leaving the decision to the jury. Juries are not perfect, and in hate crime trials there is a concern that assumptions will be made about the defendant either because of the crime charged or due to the evidence introduced at trial. . . . At the same time, the jury could be sympathetic to the defendant, or not be willing to punish the bias element of the crime.

To find a defendant guilty of a hate crime, juries must believe the defendant's motivation beyond a reasonable doubt. Compared to other crimes, even to conspiracy, this presents a very difficult dilemma. Physical evidence can conclusively establish that a defendant was at the scene of the crime. Reliable statements by witnesses can connect a defendant to a conspiracy to commit a crime. Establishing a hate crime, however, is limited to loose connections between circumstantial evidence, such as the defendant's tattoos, statements made by the defendant in anger or induced by drugs and alcohol, and prior associations with bigoted groups. These are the means by which juries are supposed to be convinced that the crime was fueled by hate.

Assessing Guilt

There are valid concerns that juries may be over-eager to punish, under-eager to do so, or may employ jury nullification. Despite this concern, however, courts have no choice but to allow the jury to play a major role following the Supreme Court's rulings in *Apprendi v. New Jersey*, *United States v. Blakely*, and *United States v. Booker*. In *Apprendi*, the Court addressed New Jersey hate crime law and recognized that given the exponential increase in sentences for biased offenders, the state should be required to prove the defendant's racial motivation to the jury beyond a reasonable doubt, not to the judge by a preponderance of the evidence as had been prescribed by the New Jersey legislature.

Blakely and *Booker* soon affirmed the holding in *Apprendi* that other than a prior conviction, any statutorily mandated element of an offense that leads to an increased punishment must be proven to a jury and cannot be left to a judge. The Court said that an element of an offense is considered essential if it presents increased punishment exposure; once there is the potential for a sentence greater than the statutorily prescribed maximum, the jury must make a determination beyond a reasonable doubt. These decisions have sought to ensure that a jury will be involved in determining every aspect of a defendant's guilt to guarantee the constitutional protection of the accused's rights. The jury's ability to assess the mind of a defendant charged with a motive-based crime has been affirmed as the major determinant of that person's fate and freedom.

Striking a Balance

The conclusion of this discussion should not be, as some have argued, that the enactment of hate crime statutes is a mistake;

their societal good is of extraordinary importance. Offsetting this benefit, however, are the risks associated with making motive an element of the offense, the imposition of mandatory sentence enhancements, and the Sixth Amendment requirements of *Booker*. Hate crime laws are acceptable because this balance is even. It is only as the continuum progresses, and the motive element becomes a greater factor in the offense, that any balance between the benefits to society and the risks to the defendant turns in favor of the accused.

Issues on Trial

Chapter 3

Victims of Gender Violence Cannot Sue Their Attackers in Federal Court

Case Overview

United States v. Morrison (2000)

In a contentious decision, the Supreme Court invalidated a law enacted by Congress that provided a civil remedy for victims of gender-motivated violence. At the center of the controversy was the Violence Against Women Act of 1994 (VAWA) that stated, "All persons within the United States shall have the right to be free from crimes of violence motivated by gender." The VAWA allowed for the victim's recovery of monetary damages and court action, such as injunctive and declaratory relief (which controlled subsequent actions of the assailant). When Congress passed the Act, it specifically identified two sources for its federal authority: the Commerce Clause and Section 5 of the Fourteenth Amendment.

The case, *United States v. Morrison*, arose from an attack—beatings and multiple rapes—on a freshman female by two Virginia Tech football players, Antonio Morrison and James Crawford. In the months following the rape, Morrison boasted of the vulgar and degrading acts he would do against women. The victim suffered emotional distress and depression as a result of the attack. She sued her assailants under the VAWA, claiming that the rapes and subsequent public threats ("gender animus") represented hate crimes.

Chief Justice William Rehnquist, ruling that Congress exceeded its powers in enacting the VAWA, declared that the Commerce Clause failed to provide sufficient authority for the law because the violence did not represent economic activity, nor did it involve interstate commerce; therefore, the results of the rapes could not be tied to a causal chain that influenced commerce. Lacking this tie to interstate commerce, asserted the Chief Justice, the federal government did not possess the essential power to regulate local crime. The Constitution distinguishes between activities that are national and those that are local—the Constitution empowers states to regulate local crime. While Section 5 of the Fourteenth Amendment grants Congress the right to enforce by legislation the guarantee that no state shall deprive any person of life, liberty, or property without due process or deny any person equal protection of the laws, the Chief Justice pointed out that the Fourteenth Amendment placed limitations on the means by which Congress regulated discriminatory conduct. Most importantly, contended the Chief Justice, the Fourteenth Amendment addressed only state action, not private conduct; accordingly, the reach of federal law could not extend to individuals who committed gender-bias crime.

The holding in *Morrison* was a divisive 5-4 decision. By ruling that Congress overstepped its powers, the Court majority never directly ruled whether rape constituted a hate crime. Still, the opinions written by other Justices emphasized major points of contention and concern. Justice Stephen Breyer opined that the issue of violence directed at women is a national problem, requiring federal intervention. He asserted that Congress, not the courts, should take responsibility for balancing state and federal legal matters. Justice David Souter, in his dissent, concluded that it should be with the powers of Congress to determine whether an action constitutes interstate commerce within the scope of the Commerce Clause. He noted that in enacting the Violence Against Women Act, Congress compiled extensive data documenting the interstate commercial impact of gender-motivated crimes of violence. To the contrary, Justice Clarence Thomas warned in his concurrence that the federal government must realize that the Commerce Clause has defined limits—the failure to keep Congress in check will result in increased federal encroachment of state police powers.

"Due respect for the decisions of a coordinate branch of Government demands that we invalidate a congressional enactment only upon a plain showing that Congress has exceeded its constitutional bounds."

The Court's Decision: Parts of the Violence Against Women Act Are Unconstitutional

William Rehnquist

In the majority ruling in United States v. Morrison, *William Rehnquist declares that Congress exceeded its authority in enacting the Violence Against Women Act of 1994 (42 U.S.C. Section 13981), which provided a federal civil remedy for victims of gender-motivated violence. The case involved a female student raped by other male college students. She sued her assailants under the Act, claiming that the rapes represented hate crimes. Congress expressly identified two sources for its federal authority in enacting the Act: the Commerce Clause and Section 5 of the Fourteenth Amendment. Rehnquist concluded that the Commerce Clause fails to provide authority for the law because the violence did not represent economic activity nor did it involve interstate commerce; therefore, the effects of the rapes could not be tied to a causal chain that influenced interstate commerce. Without the tie to commerce, he proclaims that the federal government lacks the authority to regulate local crime. While Section 5 of the Fourteenth Amendment gives Congress the right to enforce by legislation the guarantee that no state shall deprive*

William Rehnquist, majority opinion, *United States v. Morrison*, U.S. Supreme Court, 529 U.S. 598, in Legal Information Institute, Cornell University Law School, 2000.

any person of life, liberty, or property without due process or deny any person equal protection of the laws, Rehnquist notes that the Amendment places restrictions on the means by which Congress regulates discriminatory conduct. Most importantly, declares Rehnquist, the Amendment addresses only state action, not private conduct; accordingly, even if a state is guilty of gender discrimination, the reach of federal law does not extend to individuals who have committed a gender-bias crime. William H. Rehnquist was appointed to the Court in 1972 as an associate justice by President Richard Nixon. In 1986 he was elevated to Chief Justice by President Ronald Reagan. A conservative, his thirty-three years on the Court were some of the longest and most influential in Supreme Court history. He retired from the Court in 2005, shortly before his death.

Petitioner Christy Brzonkala enrolled at Virginia Polytechnic Institute (Virginia Tech) in the fall of 1994. In September of that year, Brzonkala met respondents Antonio Morrison and James Crawford, who were both students at Virginia Tech and members of its varsity football team. Brzonkala alleges that, within 30 minutes of meeting Morrison and Crawford, they assaulted and repeatedly raped her. After the attack, Morrison allegedly told Brzonkala, "You better not have any . . . diseases." In the months following the rape, Morrison also allegedly announced in the dormitory's dining room that he "like[d] to get girls drunk and . . . ." The omitted portions, quoted verbatim in the briefs on file with this Court, consist of boasting, debased remarks about what Morrison would do to women, vulgar remarks that cannot fail to shock and offend. . . .

Violence Against Women Act of 1994

Section 13981 was part of the Violence Against Women Act of 1994. It states that "[a]ll persons within the United States shall have the right to be free from crimes of violence motivated by gender." To enforce that right, subsection (c) declares:

> A person (including a person who acts under color of any statute, ordinance, regulation, custom, or usage of any State) who commits a crime of violence motivated by gender and thus deprives another of the right declared in subsection (b) of this section shall be liable to the party injured, in an action for the recovery of compensatory and punitive damages, injunctive and declaratory relief, and such other relief as a court may deem appropriate.

Section 13981 defines a "crim[e] of violence motivated by gender" as "a crime of violence committed because of gender or on the basis of gender, and due, at least in part, to an animus based on the victim's gender." It also provides that the term "crime of violence" includes any

> (A) . . . act or series of acts that would constitute a felony against the person or that would constitute a felony against property if the conduct presents a serious risk of physical injury to another, and that would come within the meaning of State or Federal offenses described in section 16 of Title 18, whether or not those acts have actually resulted in criminal charges, prosecution, or conviction and whether or not those acts were committed in the special maritime, territorial, or prison jurisdiction of the United States; and
>
> (B) includes an act or series of acts that would constitute a felony described in subparagraph (A) but for the relationship between the person who takes such action and the individual against whom such action is taken. . . .

Congressional Power over Commerce

Due respect for the decisions of a coordinate branch of Government demands that we invalidate a congressional enactment only upon a plain showing that Congress has exceeded its constitutional bounds. With this presumption of constitutionality in mind, we turn to the question whether § 13981 falls within Congress' power under Article I, § 8, of the Constitution. Brzonkala and the United States rely upon the third clause of the Article, which gives Congress power "[t]o regulate Commerce with foreign Nations, and among the several States, and with the Indian Tribes."

As we discussed at length in [*United States v. Lopez*] our interpretation of the Commerce Clause has changed as our Nation has developed. We need not repeat that detailed review of the Commerce Clause's history here; it suffices to say that, in the years since *NLRB v. Jones & Laughlin Steel Corp.* (1937), Congress has had considerably greater latitude in regulating conduct and transactions under the Commerce Clause than our previous case law permitted.

Lopez emphasized, however, that even under our modern, expansive interpretation of the Commerce Clause, Congress' regulatory authority is not without effective bounds. . . .

Scope of Commerce Clause Limited

With these principles underlying our Commerce Clause jurisprudence as reference points, the proper resolution of the present cases is clear. Gender-motivated crimes of violence are not, in any sense of the phrase, economic activity. While we need not adopt a categorical rule against aggregating the effects of any noneconomic activity in order to decide these cases, thus far in our Nation's history our cases have upheld Commerce Clause regulation of intrastate activity only where that activity is economic in nature.

Like the Gun-Free School Zones Act at issue in *Lopez*, § 13981 contains no jurisdictional element establishing that the federal cause of action is in pursuance of Congress' power to regulate interstate commerce. Although *Lopez* makes clear that such a jurisdictional element would lend support to the argument that § 13981 is sufficiently tied to interstate commerce, Congress elected to cast § 13981's remedy over a wider, and more purely intrastate, body of violent crime. . . .

In these cases, Congress' findings are substantially weakened by the fact that they rely so heavily on a method of reasoning that we have already rejected as unworkable if we are to maintain the Constitution's enumeration of powers. Congress found that gender-motivated violence affects interstate commerce

> by deterring potential victims from traveling interstate, from engaging in employment in interstate business, and from transacting with business, and in places involved in interstate commerce; . . . by diminishing national productivity, increasing medical and other costs, and decreasing the supply of and the demand for interstate products. . . .

National Versus Local Commerce

We accordingly reject the argument that Congress may regulate noneconomic, violent criminal conduct based solely on that conduct's aggregate effect on interstate commerce. The Constitution requires a distinction between what is truly national and what is truly local. In recognizing this fact we preserve one of the few principles that has been consistent since the Clause was adopted. The regulation and punishment of intrastate violence that is not directed at the instrumentalities, channels, or goods involved in interstate commerce has always been the province of the States. Indeed, we can think of no better example of the police power, which the Founders denied the National Government and reposed in the States, than the suppression of violent crime and vindication of its victims.

Fourteenth Amendment

Because we conclude that the Commerce Clause does not provide Congress with authority to enact § 13981, we address petitioners' alternative argument that the section's civil remedy should be upheld as an exercise of Congress' remedial power under § 5 of the Fourteenth Amendment. As noted above, Congress expressly invoked the Fourteenth Amendment as a source of authority to enact § 13981.

The principles governing an analysis of congressional legislation under § 5 are well settled. Section 5 states that Congress may "'enforce,' by 'appropriate legislation' the constitutional guarantee that no State shall deprive any person of 'life, liberty or property, without due process or law,' nor deny any person 'equal protection of the laws'" [*City of Boerne v. Flores*, 1997]. In fact, as we discuss in detail below, several limitations inherent in § 5's text and constitutional context have been recognized since the Fourteenth Amendment was adopted.

Section 5

Petitioners' § 5 argument is founded on an assertion that there is pervasive bias in various state justice systems against victims of gender-motivated violence. This assertion is supported by a voluminous congressional record. Specifically, Congress received evidence that many participants in state justice systems are perpetuating an array of erroneous stereotypes and assumptions. Congress concluded that these discriminatory stereotypes often result in insufficient investigation and prosecution of gender-motivated crime, inappropriate focus on the behavior and credibility of the victims of that crime, and unacceptably lenient punishments for those who are actually convicted of gender-motivated violence. Petitioners contend that this bias denies victims of gender-motivated violence the equal protection of the laws and that Congress therefore acted appropriately in enacting a private civil remedy against the perpetrators of gender-motivated violence to both remedy the States' bias and deter future instances of discrimination in the state courts.

Equal Protection

As our cases have established, state-sponsored gender discrimination violates equal protection unless it serves "important governmental objectives and . . . the discriminatory means employed" are "substantially related to the achievement of those objectives" [*United States v. Virginia*, 1996]. However, the language and purpose of the Fourteenth Amendment place certain limitations on the manner in which Congress may attack discriminatory conduct. These limitations are necessary to prevent the Fourteenth Amendment from obliterating the Framers' carefully crafted balance of power between the States and the National Government. Foremost among these limitations is the time-honored principle that the Fourteenth Amendment, by its very terms, prohibits only state action. "[T]he principle has become firmly embedded in our constitutional law that the action inhibited by the first section of the Fourteenth Amendment is only such action as may fairly be said to be that of the States. That Amendment erects no shield against merely private conduct, however discriminatory or wrongful" [*Shelley v. Kraemer*, 1948].

Supporting Cases

Shortly after the Fourteenth Amendment was adopted, we decided two cases interpreting the Amendment's provisions, *United States v. Harris* (1883), and the *Civil Rights Cases* (1883). In *Harris*, the Court considered a challenge to § 2 of the Civil Rights Act of 1871. That section sought to punish "private persons" for "conspiring to deprive any one of the equal protection of the laws enacted by the State." We concluded that this law exceeded Congress' § 5 power because the law was "directed exclusively against the action of private persons, without reference to the laws of the State, or their administration by her officers." In so doing, we reemphasized our statement from *Virginia v. Rives* (1880) that "'these provisions of the fourteenth amendment have reference to State action exclusively, and not to any action of private individuals.'"

We reached a similar conclusion in the *Civil Rights Cases*. In those consolidated cases, we held that the public accommodation provisions of the Civil Rights Act of 1875, which applied to purely private conduct, were beyond the scope of the

§ 5 enforcement power. ("Individual invasion of individual rights is not the subject-matter of the [Fourteenth] [A]mendment.")

The force of the doctrine of *stare decisis* [to abide by decided case law] behind these decisions stems not only from the length of time they have been on the books, but also from the insight attributable to the Members of the Court at that time. Every Member had been appointed by President [Abraham] Lincoln, [Ulysses S.] Grant, [Rutherford B.] Hayes, [James] Garfield or [Chester] Arthur—and each of their judicial appointees obviously had intimate knowledge and familiarity with the events surrounding the adoption of the Fourteenth Amendment. . . .

Gender Discrimination

Petitioners alternatively argue that, unlike the situation in the *Civil Rights Cases*, here there has been gender-based disparate treatment by state authorities, whereas in those cases there was no indication of such state action. There is abundant evidence, however, to show that the Congresses that enacted the Civil Rights Acts of 1871 and 1875 had a purpose similar to that of Congress in enacting § 13981: There were state laws on the books bespeaking equality of treatment, but in the administration of these laws there was discrimination against newly freed slaves. . . .

Section 13981 is not aimed at proscribing discrimination by officials which the Fourteenth Amendment might not itself proscribe; it is directed not at any State or state actor, but at individuals who have committed criminal acts motivated by gender bias.

In the present cases, for example, § 13981 visits no consequence whatever on any Virginia public official involved in investigating or prosecuting Brzonkala's assault. The section is, therefore, unlike any of the § 5 remedies that we have previously upheld. For example, in *Katzenbach v. Morgan* (1966),

Congress prohibited New York from imposing literacy tests as a prerequisite for voting because it found that such a requirement disenfranchised thousands of Puerto Rican immigrants who had been educated in the Spanish language of their home territory. That law, which we upheld, was directed at New York officials who administered the State's election law and prohibited them from using a provision of that law. In *South Carolina v. Katzenbach* (1966), Congress imposed voting rights requirements on States that, Congress found, had a history of discriminating against blacks in voting. The remedy was also directed at state officials in those States. Similarly, in *Ex parte Virginia* (1880), Congress criminally punished state officials who intentionally discriminated in jury selection; again, the remedy was directed to the culpable state official.

Section 13981 is also different from these previously upheld remedies in that it applies uniformly throughout the Nation. Congress' findings indicate that the problem of discrimination against the victims of gender-motivated crimes does not exist in all States, or even most States. By contrast, the § 5 remedy upheld in *Katzenbach v. Morgan, supra*, was directed only to the State where the evil found by Congress existed, and in *South Carolina v. Katzenbach, supra*, the remedy was directed only to those States in which Congress found that there had been discrimination.

Congress Exceeded Its Powers

For these reasons, we conclude that Congress' power under § 5 does not extend to the enactment of § 13981.

Petitioner Brzonkala's complaint alleges that she was the victim of a brutal assault. But Congress' effort in § 13981 to provide a federal civil remedy can be sustained neither under the Commerce Clause nor under § 5 of the Fourteenth Amendment. If the allegations here are true, no civilized system of justice could fail to provide her a remedy for the conduct of respondent Morrison. But under our federal system

that remedy must be provided by the Commonwealth of Virginia, and not by the United States.

"The law before us seems to represent an instance, not of state/federal conflict, but of state/federal efforts to cooperate in order to help solve a mutually acknowledged national problem."

Dissenting Opinion: The Court's Ruling Is Underinclusive

Stephen Breyer

In United States v. Morrison *the Court ruled that parts of the Violence Against Women Act, which allowed victims of gender violence to sue their attackers in federal court, are unconstitutional. In the following dissenting opinion, Stephen Breyer declares that the issue of violence directed at women is national in scope, requiring federal resources. Breyer recognizes the importance of the division of authority between state and federal governments. However, he states that the distinctions between economic and noneconomic activities under the Commerce Clause are difficult to separate and apply. He asserts that Congress, not the courts, should take responsibility for balancing state and federal matters. In enacting the Violence Against Women Act of 1994, Congress compiled extensive data documenting the interstate commercial impact of gender-motivated crimes of violence. The Justice concludes that the Act is within the authority of Congress under the Commerce Clause. Justice Breyer also disagrees with the majority opinion in its rejection of the Fourteenth Amendment Section 5 rationale since the cases relied*

Stephen Breyer, dissenting opinion, *United States v. Morrison*, U.S. Supreme Court, 529 U.S. 598, in Legal Information Institute, Cornell University Law School, 2000.

upon by the majority did not specifically consider the kind of claims addressed by the Act. Also, he contends, a number of states lack adequate legal remedies for gender hate crimes that the Act specifically addresses. Stephen Breyer was appointed to the Supreme Court in 1994 by President Bill Clinton.

No one denies the importance of the Constitution's federalist principles. Its state/federal division of authority protects liberty—both by restricting the burdens that government can impose from a distance and by facilitating citizen participation in government that is closer to home. The question is how the judiciary can best implement that original federalist understanding where the Commerce Clause is at issue.

The majority holds that the federal commerce power does not extend to such "noneconomic" activities as "noneconomic, violent criminal conduct" that significantly affects interstate commerce only if we "aggregate" the interstate "effect[s]" of individual instances. Justice Souter explains why history, precedent, and legal logic militate against the majority's approach. I agree and join his opinion. I add that the majority's holding illustrates the difficulty of finding a workable judicial Commerce Clause touchstone—a set of comprehensible interpretive rules that courts might use to impose some meaningful limit, but not too great a limit, upon the scope of the legislative authority that the Commerce Clause delegates to Congress.

Unworkable Distinction

Consider the problems. The "economic/noneconomic" distinction is not easy to apply. Does the local street corner mugger engage in "economic" activity or "noneconomic" activity when he mugs for money?. . . Would evidence that desire for economic domination underlies many brutal crimes against women save the present statute?

The line becomes yet harder to draw given the need for exceptions. The Court itself would permit Congress to aggregate, hence regulate, "noneconomic" activity taking place at economic establishments.

More important, why should we give critical constitutional importance to the economic, or noneconomic, nature of an interstate-commerce-affecting *cause*? If chemical emanations through indirect environmental change cause identical, severe commercial harm outside a State, why should it matter whether local factories or home fireplaces release them? The Constitution itself refers only to Congress' power to "regulate Commerce . . . among the several States," and to make laws "necessary and proper" to implement that power. The language says nothing about either the local nature, or the economic nature, of an interstate-commerce-affecting cause.

This Court has long held that only the interstate commercial effects, not the local nature of the cause, are constitutionally relevant. Nothing in the Constitution's language, or that of earlier cases prior to *Lopez* [*United States v. Lopez* (1995)], explains why the Court should ignore one highly relevant characteristic of an interstate-commerce-affecting cause (how "local" it is), while placing critical constitutional weight upon a different, less obviously relevant, feature (how "economic" it is).

Most important, the Court's complex rules seem unlikely to help secure the very object that they seek, namely, the protection of "areas of traditional state regulation" from federal intrusion. The Court's rules, even if broadly interpreted, are underinclusive. The local pickpocket is no less a traditional subject of state regulation than is the local gender-motivated assault. Regardless, the Court reaffirms, as it should, Congress' well-established and frequently exercised power to enact laws that satisfy a commerce-related jurisdictional prerequisite—for example, that some item relevant to the federally regulated activity has at some time crossed a state line. . . .

Defining Interstate Commerce

And in a world where most everyday products or their component parts cross interstate boundaries, Congress will frequently find it possible to redraft a statute using language that ties the regulation to the interstate movement of some relevant object, thereby regulating local criminal activity or, for that matter, family affairs. Although this possibility does not give the Federal Government the power to regulate everything, it means that any substantive limitation will apply randomly in terms of the interests the majority seeks to protect. How much would be gained, for example, were Congress to reenact the present law in the form of "An Act Forbidding Violence Against Women Perpetrated at Public Accommodations or by Those Who Have Moved in, or through the Use of Items that Have Moved in, Interstate Commerce"? Complex Commerce Clause rules creating fine distinctions that achieve only random results do little to further the important federalist interests that called them into being.

The majority, aware of these difficulties, is nonetheless concerned with what it sees as an important contrary consideration. To determine the lawfulness of statutes simply by asking whether Congress could reasonably have found that *aggregated* local instances significantly affect interstate commerce will allow Congress to regulate almost anything. . . .

Effects on Commerce Widespread

We live in a Nation knit together by two centuries of scientific, technological, commercial, and environmental change. Those changes, taken together, mean that virtually every kind of activity, no matter how local, genuinely can affect commerce, or its conditions, outside the State—at least when considered in the aggregate. And that fact makes it close to impossible for courts to develop meaningful subject-matter categories that would exclude some kinds of local activities from ordinary Commerce Clause "aggregation" rules without, at the same time, depriving Congress of the power to regulate activities that have a genuine and important effect upon interstate commerce.

Congress Most Able to Balance State and Federal Matters

Since judges cannot change the world, the "defect" means that, within the bounds of the rational, Congress, not the courts, must remain primarily responsible for striking the appropriate state/federal balance. Congress is institutionally motivated to do so. Its Members represent state and local district interests. They consider the views of state and local officials when they legislate, and they have even developed formal procedures to ensure that such consideration takes place. Moreover, Congress often can better reflect state concerns for autonomy in the details of sophisticated statutory schemes than can the judiciary, which cannot easily gather the relevant facts and which must apply more general legal rules and categories. Not surprisingly, the bulk of American law is still state law, and overwhelmingly so.

I would also note that Congress, when it enacted the statute, followed procedures that help to protect the federalism values at stake. . . .

Moreover, as Justice Souter has pointed out, Congress compiled a "mountain of data" explicitly documenting the interstate commercial effects of gender-motivated crimes of violence. After considering alternatives, it focused the federal law upon documented deficiencies in state legal systems. And it tailored the law to prevent its use in certain areas of traditional state concern, such as divorce, alimony, or child custody. Consequently, the law before us seems to represent an instance, not of state/federal conflict, but of state/federal efforts to cooperate in order to help solve a mutually acknowledged national problem.

I recognize that the law in this area is unstable and that time and experience may demonstrate both the unworkability of the majority's rules and the superiority of Congress' own procedural approach—in which case the law may evolve towards a rule that, in certain difficult Commerce Clause cases, takes account of the thoroughness with which Congress has considered the federalism issue.

For these reasons, as well as those set forth by Justice Souter, this statute falls well within Congress's Commerce Clause authority, and I dissent from the Court's contrary conclusion.

Application for Section 5

Given my conclusion on the Commerce Clause question, I need not consider Congress' authority under § 5 of the Fourteenth Amendment. Nonetheless, I doubt the Court's reasoning rejecting that source of authority. The Court points out that in *United States v. Harris* (1883) and the *Civil Rights Cases* (1883), the Court held that § 5 does not authorize Congress to use the Fourteenth Amendment as a source of power to remedy the conduct of *private persons*. That is certainly so. The Federal Government's argument, however, is that Congress used § 5 to remedy the actions of *state actors*, namely, those States which, through discriminatory design or the discriminatory conduct of their officials, failed to provide adequate (or any) state remedies for women injured by gender-motivated violence—a failure that the States, and Congress, documented in depth.

Neither *Harris* nor the *Civil Rights Cases* considered this kind of claim. The Court in *Harris* specifically said that it treated the federal laws in question as "directed *exclusively* against the action of private persons, without reference to the laws of the State, or their administration by her officers." See also *Civil Rights Cases* (observing that the statute did "not profess to be corrective of any constitutional wrong committed by the States" and that it established "rules for the conduct of individuals in society towards each other, . . . without referring in any manner to any supposed action of the State or its authorities").

Adequacy of State Remedies

The majority adds that Congress found that the problem of inadequacy of state remedies "does not exist in all States, or even most States." But Congress had before it the task force reports of at least 21 States documenting constitutional violations. And it made its own findings about pervasive gender-based stereotypes hampering many state legal systems, sometimes unconstitutionally so. The record nowhere reveals a congressional finding that the problem "does not exist" elsewhere. Why can Congress not take the evidence before it as evidence of a national problem? This Court has not previously held that Congress must document the existence of a problem in every State prior to proposing a national solution. And the deference this Court gives to Congress' chosen remedy under § 5 suggests that any such requirement would be inappropriate.

Despite my doubts about the majority's § 5 reasoning, I need not, and do not, answer the § 5 question, which I would leave for more thorough analysis if necessary on another occasion. Rather, in my view, the Commerce Clause provides an adequate basis for the statute before us. And I would uphold its constitutionality as the "necessary and proper" exercise of legislative power granted to Congress by that Clause.

"The Court's holding in Morrison *predictably limited the power of Congress to regulate local crime."*

Morrison Limits Attempts by Congress to Regulate Local Hate Crime

Bernard P. Haggerty

In this viewpoint, Bernard Haggerty suggests that Congress should be permitted to provide a federal remedy for hate crimes in areas that fail to cooperate with HCSA (Hate Crime Statistics Act), despite the ruling by the Supreme Court in United States v. Morrison. *The Court in* Morrison *ruled that a federal law regulating gender-based hate crimes was invalid since the law was erroneously based on Commerce Clause and Fourteenth Amendment support. However, notes Haggerty, Congress possesses the duty and power to protect against discriminatory crimes. HCSA seeks to collect statistics on state crimes that indicate evidence of prejudice based on race, disability, religion, sexual orientation, or ethnicity. Another method by which Congress regulates some hate crime activity includes the Hate Crimes Sentencing Enhancement Act, which provides guidelines for sentencing enhancement for federal hate crimes. Haggerty concludes that the proposed federal hate crime regulation—the Hate Crimes Prevention Act (HCPA)—would give Congress nationwide power against state discriminatory interference and add*

Bernard P. Haggerty, "Hate Crimes: A View from Laramie, Wyoming's First Bias Crime Law, the Fight Against Discriminatory Crime and a New Cooperative Federalism," *Howard Law Journal*, Fall 2001. Reproduced by permission.

gender, sexual orientation, and disability as prohibited biases. Bernard Haggerty is a former law professor and member of Wyoming Attorney General's Hate Crime Training Group.

In states or localities that have demonstrated insufficient cooperation with the HCSA [Hate Crime Statistics Act], Congress should provide both a federal criminal penalty for hate crimes and a federal civil rights remedy to victims of hate crimes. Such a civil rights remedy was stricken in *United States v. Morrison* because it was not justified by either a specific Commerce Clause nexus or Fourteenth Amendment authority. Congress, however, possesses implicit authority to mandate compliance with an inquiry into the scope and nature of discriminatory crime, under either the Commerce Clause or the Fourteenth Amendment, at least in jurisdictions that refuse to cooperate with, or misapply, the HCSA. Congress also has a duty to provide a national minimum of protection against discriminatory crime.

Existing Federal Regulation of Hate Crime

In addition to general civil and criminal anti-discrimination laws, and state hate crime laws, the federal government regulates some hate crime activity. First, the HCSA encourages local police to gather statistics about state crimes that "manifest evidence of prejudice based on race, religion, disability, sexual orientation, or ethnicity." Second, the Hate Crimes Sentencing Enhancement Act and the implementing guidelines of the United States Sentencing Commission authorize sentence enhancements for federal crimes where "the defendant intentionally selected any victim . . . because of the actual or perceived race, color, religion, national origin, ethnicity, gender, disability, or sexual orientation of any person."

Hate Crimes Prevention Act

A third mode of federal hate crime regulation has been proposed. The Hate Crimes Prevention Act (HCPA) would convert the existing federal statute criminalizing the discriminatory interference with "federally protected activities" into a nationwide hate crime law. In addition to eliminating the "federally protected activities" limitation, the HCPA would add sexual orientation, gender, and disability as prohibited biases. Proponents of the HCPA would incorporate a "backstop" permitting federal prosecution if the Attorney General certifies that it is "in the public interest and necessary to secure substantial justice." The purpose of this self-imposed limit is to preserve a spirit of cooperation with state and local police:

It is precisely because we are in an era of cooperative federalism with respect to hate crime that it is such a good idea to fine-tune the federal backstop to assure that the full resources of every level of government can be brought to bear on the scourge of violence engendered by group hatred.

Aside from the HCSA, however, there is currently no federal hate crime law applicable to state law crimes. Hence, in states like Wyoming, which lack any hate crime law, only federal crimes are subject to sentence enhancement for a discriminatory intent.

Proponents of the HCPA cite several deficiencies in existing hate crime regulation. First, state hate crime laws lack uniformity and are not always enforced.

Second, existing federal remedies are subject to self-imposed statutory limitations such as, for example, the limitation to federally protected activities and limitations on the types of discrimination regulated.

Finally, in addition to self-imposed statutory limitations modern hate crime legislation is also subject to constitutional limitations.

Modern Limits on the Power of Congress

Even before the Court's decision in *Morrison*, commentators emphasized the importance of that decision to future federal hate crime legislation. The Court's holding in *Morrison* predictably limited the power of Congress to regulate local crime. The Court stated, "Congress may [not] regulate non-economic, violent criminal conduct based solely on that conduct's aggregate effect on interstate commerce." Before *Morrison*, Congress possessed three modes of Commerce Clause power under which it could regulate: (a) channels of interstate commerce; (b) instrumentalities of, and persons or things in, interstate commerce; and (c) activities substantially affecting interstate commerce. The Court in *Morrison* restricted the third mode, holding that traditional state police powers, such as "the suppression of violent crime and the vindication of its victims," are categorically excluded from regulation, regardless of any aggregate effects of an activity on commerce. Congress can thus create federal civil and criminal causes of action in these traditional state areas only by limiting its legislation to the first two modes of regulation—by making a specific commerce nexus either an element of proof or a prerequisite in a separate jurisdictional provision.

Commerce Clause

Before *Morrison*, Congress could attempt to justify its exercise of Commerce Clause power in a three-step process. First, Congress would identify a specific problem, for example, gender discrimination in state civil and criminal remedies. Second, it would show that the activity being regulated is a national problem. Third, Congress would show that the national problem, in the aggregate, affects interstate commerce. The HCSA is tailor-made to supply information about the first two inquiries; however, because *Morrison* makes the third inquiry futile, at least under the Commerce Clause, the HCSA has lost much of its utility.

Under *Morrison*, any federal hate crime law—whether a federal criminal or civil rights remedy for hate crimes—will be similarly limited. Even a mountain of statistics cannot expand federal hate crime legislation beyond those cases involving a specific commerce nexus. Therefore, at least for purposes of the Court's current aggregate effects Commerce Clause analysis, *Morrison* appears to render the HCSA pointless.

Critics of the VAWA [Violence Against Women Act of 1994] noted that the civil rights remedy at issue in *Morrison* would be merely symbolic because state suits for assault are already available to victims, and because many defendants would be judgment-proof. On the other hand, the federal civil rights remedy permitted an alternative to the local state court forum, and empowered victims by authorizing attorney fees.

Section 5, Fourteenth Amendment

Morrison also addressed the limits of the enforcement power in Section 5 of the Fourteenth Amendment. The Court held that the Fourteenth Amendment did not authorize the civil remedy provision of the VAWA for three reasons: (1) it reached beyond the state action limitation to regulate purely private conduct; (2) it was not adapted to cure discrimination by state officials; and (3) it was not geographically tailored to apply only in those states that exhibited discrimination.

Assuming a national hate crime civil or criminal remedy could overcome the first two limitations, which would require careful drafting in light of *Morrison*, the HCSA would supply information relevant to the third requirement—narrow geographic tailoring. Yet, by what authority might Congress compel states to disclose information about their discriminatory practices? If state or local authorities refuse to inquire into the discriminatory motives of suspects and refuse to disclose the bias motivations of crimes within their jurisdictions, as is the case in at least parts of Wyoming, then Congress has no meaningful way to tailor a Fourteenth Amendment response to bias crimes.

"The question we face is if the federal government should have the power to lock people away for beliefs flowing from their religion. . . . We punish people for their wrong acts, not for what some consider their wrong thoughts."

To Fight Hatred, Don't Over-Legislate Hate Crimes

Kenneth Blackwell

In the following article, Kenneth Blackwell discusses the Local Law Enforcement Hate Crimes Prevention Act of 2007, a bill that would place suspected hate crimes under federal jurisdiction. The author contends that this proposed law is seemingly unconstitutional, as it punishes and seeks to "prove" a person's opinion rather than merely his actions. Kenneth Blackwell is a contributing editor of Townhall.com and a senior fellow at both the Family Research Council and the Buckeye Institute.

> "[T]he legitimate powers of government reach actions only and not opinions."
>
> —*Thomas Jefferson*

For those who commit physical crimes against others based on race, religion, or sexual orientation I have no sympathy. But the notion that government can punish thoughts and opinions, even offensive ones, is frightening.

Local Law Enforcement Hate Crimes Prevention Act

A bill that makes it illegal for persons of various faiths to freely hold and profess their religion's teaching on sexual morality is working its way through Congress.

Regardless of your politics, every American who cares about free speech and religious liberty should tell their senators to oppose this legislation. This bill has already passed the House of Representatives on a largely party-line vote with a Democrat majority. It is now pending in the Senate Judiciary Committee, and is expected to be voted on by the entire Senate in a month.

This bill would criminalize beliefs. If signed into law, H.R. 1592 would create a new class of crimes. Called the Local Law Enforcement Hate Crimes Prevention Act of 2007, this bill would pour federal resources into prosecutions based on suspicions about a person's thoughts and beliefs, not just his alleged criminal act(s).

While criminal law treats all violent acts equally, the proposed law would additionally punish the accused for any prejudice they might have toward the victim. Instead of ending discrimination, this bill would create a judicial caste system in American society by creating categories where some victims are given more consideration and attention than others. This is a direct affront to the equal protection provision of our constitution.

As a former U.S. Ambassador to the U.N. Human Rights Commission, and a person who grew up fighting racism, I oppose the idea of thought crimes. In America, our Constitution guarantees everyone the freedom to think and believe whatever he or she wants, no matter how repulsive those beliefs are to others. And, our Declaration of Independence champions the dignity and worth of every individual.

Our system of laws requires evidence and varying levels of proof for different offenses. We lock people up for criminal acts. That penalty is already established in law. This bill would allow government to further punish them for their alleged beliefs.

Denying Freedom of Opinion

As a country, do we want to be in the business of "proving" what someone thinks or denying them freedom of conscience? Do we want to rip the heart out of the First Amendment of our Constitution? Do we want to deconstruct our public square where progress has been advanced by a dialogue between faith and reason? Do we really want to embolden a 21st-century secular fundamentalism by forcing religious expression from the public square?

The answer to these questions is a simple and emphatic no.

What is driving the controversy associated with this bill ultimately comes down to one issue: Can the government punish a person for a "thought crime" whose religious faith includes the belief that homosexual behavior is immoral and that same-sex marriage is morally objectionable?

While some modern liberal denominations and other faiths embrace same-sex marriage and refuse to criticize homosexual sex, it is an historical fact that moral evaluations of these acts have been part of the Judeo-Christian belief system for 4,000 years. Millions of Americans oppose these acts because they believe the historic teachings of their respective religions on this matter.

They are equally free to believe this just as one is free to disagree with it.

No rational person argues against the proposition that all American citizens should be afforded full rights and protections under the law and Constitution. The present debate surrounding this bill is derived from the fight to preserve the most fundamental institution—the family—necessary for the continuation of any human civilization.

Isn't it classic community doublespeak when a society that has decriminalized homosexuality is now contemplating criminalizing opposition thoughts?

The question we face is if the federal government should have the power to lock people away for beliefs flowing from their religion. Think it can't happen?

In Sweden, a pastor was imprisoned for 30 days for simply expressing his faith's view of homosexuality in a sermon. In Canada, Christian leaders received a hefty fine for expressing the same view over the radio. And right here in America, in Philadelphia, 11 people were arrested and prosecuted for sharing the Christian gospel at a homosexual rally.

No violence was committed in any of these situations. They were simply punished for expressing their faith.

Punish for Acts, Not Thought

President Bush has said he will veto this bill if it passes the Senate. Regardless of what you think about homosexuality, you should support stopping this bill.

We punish people for their wrong acts, not for what some consider their wrong thoughts. America has a rich heritage of religious liberty and free speech. Let's keep it this way.

Chapter 4

Affirming States' Rights to Ban Cross Burning Intended to Intimidate

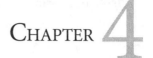

Case Overview

Virginia v. Black (2003)

The Supreme Court revisited the cross-burning issue and its conflict with the First Amendment's Free Speech Clause in *Virginia v. Black*. Unlike its predecessor, *R.A.V. v. City of St. Paul*, this decision focused specifically on the act of burning a cross, as well as the Virginia statute that outlawed this act. In upholding the statute, Justice Sandra Day O'Connor held that states are allowed to ban cross burnings that are intended to intimidate observers.

Two unrelated cross burning incidents in Virginia gave rise to the High Court case. In the first, defendants Elliot and O'Mara burned a cross in the front yard of African American James Jubilee, supposedly in response to a complaint by Jubilee against Elliot, his next-door neighbor, who fired shots behind the Elliot home. Four months later, Barry Elton Black, the Imperial Wizard of the Keystone Knights of the Ku Klux Klan, led a Klan rally held by permission on private property. The offenders were arrested and convicted under Virginia's fifty-year-old law prohibiting cross burning "with the intent of intimidating any person or group of persons" on public or private property. The law also stated: "Any such burning of a cross shall be prima facie evidence [evidence that establishes a fact or raises a presumption of a fact] of intent to intimidate a person or group of persons."

Justice O'Connor described cross burning in America as a menace intertwined with the reign of terror instigated by the Ku Klux Klan, which dated to the post-Civil War Reconstruction Era. The Justice also contended that the decision did not contradict *R.A.V. v. City of St. Paul*, since that case did not hold that the First Amendment prohibited all forms of content-based speech. Like obscenity, the Justice reasoned, a state may outlaw only those forms of intimidation most likely to instill fear of bodily harm. Moreover, the Justice declared invalid the prima facie evidence provision in the Virginia law that required a finding of intent to intimidate no matter the particular facts of the case.

Although *Virginia v. Black* was a 6–3 majority decision, it contained a plurality ruling within the majority regarding the prima facie evidence issue; furthermore, it included a concurrence, a dissent, and two opinions concurring in part and dissenting in part. For instance, Justice Clarence Thomas agreed with the validity of the Virginia statute, but concluded that all cross burnings were intimidating and should be outside the protection of the First Amendment. Meanwhile, Justices David Souter, Ruth Bader Ginsburg, and Anthony Kennedy stated the Virginia statute violated the Free Speech Clause and contradicted *R.A.V. v. City of St. Paul.* The splintered viewpoints demonstrate the difficulty of balancing individual and societal interests with the right of free speech—speech and expression that may include menacing and hateful messages that portend serious harm.

"When a cross burning is used to intimidate, few if any messages are more powerful."

The Court's Decision: Right of States to Ban Cross Burning Is Not a Violation of Free Speech

Sandra Day O'Connor

In a 6–3 majority ruling that allows states to ban cross burnings that are intended to intimidate observers, Sandra O'Connor stated that such laws do not violate the free speech rights of the First Amendment since cross burning has an extensive American history of gruesome violence. The case arose from two separate cross-burning incidents in Virginia. The Justice contends that the decision does not contradict the 1992 ruling in R.A.V. v. City of St. Paul, *since that case did not hold that the First Amendment prohibits all forms of content-based speech. Like obscenity, the Justice reasoned, a state may proscribe only the most obscene content, just as a state may proscribe only those forms of intimidation that are most likely to instill fear of bodily harm. Accordingly, Justice O'Connor depicted cross burning in America as a horror intertwined with the reign of terror instigated by the Ku Klux Klan, which dated to post-Civil War Reconstruction Era. Furthermore, in a plurality of four within the majority, the Justice declared invalid the prima facie evidence provision in the Virginia law (evidence that would, if uncontested, establish a fact or raise a presumption of a fact) that required a finding of intimidation no matter the particular facts of the case. Sandra*

Sandra Day O'Connor, majority opinion, *Virginia v. Black et al.*, U.S. Supreme Court, 538 U.S. 343, in Legal Information Institute, Cornell University Law School, 2003.

Day O'Connor, the first woman on the Supreme Court, was appointed to the Court in 1981 by President Ronald Reagan. A centrist, she served on the Court until her retirement in 2006.

In this case we consider whether the Commonwealth of Virginia's statute banning cross burning with "an intent to intimidate a person or group of persons" violates the First Amendment [Va. Code Ann. § 18.2-423 (1996)]. We conclude that while a State, consistent with the First Amendment, may ban cross burning carried out with the intent to intimidate, the provision in the Virginia statute treating any cross burning as prima facie [literally "as the first appearance"] evidence of intent to intimidate renders the statute unconstitutional in its current form.

Respondents Barry Black, Richard Elliott, and Jonathan O'Mara were convicted separately of violating Virginia's cross-burning statute, § 18.2-423. That statute provides:

> "It shall be unlawful for any person or persons, with the intent of intimidating any person or group of persons, to burn, or cause to be burned, a cross on the property of another, a highway or other public place. Any person who shall violate any provision of this section shall be guilty of a Class 6 felony. . . .
>
> Any such burning of a cross shall be prima facie evidence of an intent to intimidate a person or group of persons. . . ."

Origins of Cross Burning

Cross burning originated in the 14th century as a means for Scottish tribes to signal each other. Sir Walter Scott used cross burnings for dramatic effect in "The Lady of the Lake," where the burning cross signified both a summons and a call to arms. Cross burning in this country, however, long ago became unmoored from its Scottish ancestry. Burning a cross in the United States is inextricably intertwined with the history of the Ku Klux Klan.

The first Ku Klux Klan began in Pulaski, Tennessee, in the spring of 1866. Although the Ku Klux Klan started as a social club, it soon changed into something far different. The Klan fought Reconstruction and the corresponding drive to allow freed blacks to participate in the political process. Soon the Klan imposed "a veritable reign of terror" throughout the South. The Klan employed tactics such as whipping, threatening to burn people at the stake, and murder. The Klan's victims included blacks, southern whites who disagreed with the Klan, and "carpetbagger" northern whites.

The activities of the Ku Klux Klan promoted legislative action at the national level. . . . President Grant used . . . [powers enacted by Congress through the Ku Klux Klan Act] to suppress the Klan in South Carolina, the effect of which severely curtailed the Klan in other States as well. By the end of Reconstruction in 1877, the first Klan no longer existed.

Ideology of the Ku Klux Klan

The genesis of the second Klan began in 1905, with the publication of Thomas Dixon's *The Clansmen: An Historical Romance of the Ku Klux Klan.* Dixon's book was a sympathetic portrait of the first Klan, depicting the Klan as a group of heroes "saving" the South from blacks and "horrors" of Reconstruction. Although the first Klan never actually practiced cross burning, Dixon's book depicted the Klan burning crosses to celebrate the execution of former slaves. . . . Soon thereafter, in November 1915, the second Klan began.

From the inception of the second Klan, cross burnings have been used to communicate both threats of violence and messages of shared ideology. The first initiation ceremony occurred on Stone Mountain near Atlanta, Georgia. While a 40-foot cross burned on the mountain, the Klan members took their oaths of loyalty. This cross burning was the second recorded instance in the United States. The first known cross burning in the country had occurred a little over one month before the Klan initiation, when a Georgia mob celebrated the lynching of Leo Frank by burning a "gigantic cross" on Stone Mountain that was "visible throughout" Atlanta.

The new Klan's ideology did not differ much from that of the first Klan. . . . Violence was also an elemental part of this new Klan. By September 1921, the *New York World* newspaper documented 152 acts of Klan violence, including 4 murders, 41 floggings, and 27 tar-and-featherings.

Tools of Intimidation

Often, the Klan used cross burnings as a tool of intimidation and a threat of impending violence. For example, in 1939 and 1940, the Klan burned crosses in front of synagogues and churches. . . .

The Klan continued to use cross burning to intimidate after World War II. In one incident, [reported in 1949 by the Richmond News Leader] an African-American "school teacher who recently moved his family into a block formerly occupied only by whites asked the protection of city police . . . after the burning of a cross in his front yard." And after a cross burning in Suffolk, Virginia during the late 1940's, the Virginia Governor stated that he would "not allow any of our people of any race to be subjected to terrorism or intimidation in any form by the Klan or any other organization." These incidents of cross burning, among others, helped prompt Virginia to enact its first version of the cross-burning statute in 1950.

The decision of this Court in *Brown v. Board of Education*, (1954), along with the civil rights movement of the 1950s and 1960s, sparked another outbreak of Klan violence. These acts of violence included bombings, beatings, shootings, stabbings, and mutilations. Members of the Klan burned crosses on the lawns of those associated with the civil rights movement, assaulted the Freedom Riders, bombed churches, and murdered blacks as well as whites whom the Klan viewed as sympathetic toward the civil rights movement.

Other Meanings of Cross Burnings

Throughout the history of the Klan, cross burnings have also remained potent symbols of shared group identity and ideology. The burning cross became a symbol of the Klan itself and a central feature of Klan gatherings. According to the Klan constitution (called the Kloran), the "fiery cross" was the "emblem of that sincere, unselfish devotedness of all klansmen to the sacred purpose and principles we have espoused." And the Klan has often published its newsletters and magazines under the name *The Fiery Cross.*

At Klan gatherings across the country, cross burning became the climax of the rally or the initiation. Posters advertising an upcoming Klan rally often featured a Klan member holding a cross. Typically, a cross burning would start with a prayer by the "Klavern" minister, followed by the singing of "Onward Christian Soldiers." The Klan would then light the cross on fire, as the members raised their left arm toward the burning cross and sang "The Old Rugged Cross." Throughout the Klan's history, the Klan continued to use the burning cross in their ritual ceremonies.

For its own members, the cross was a sign of celebration and ceremony. During a joint Nazi-Klan rally in 1940, the proceeding concluded with the wedding of two Klan members [under a burning cross]. . . . In response to antimasking bills introduced in state legislatures after World War II, the Klan burned crosses in protest. . . . And cross burnings featured prominently in Klan rallies when the Klan attempted to move toward more nonviolent tactics to stop integration. In short, a burning cross has remained a symbol of Klan ideology and of Klan unity.

Symbol of Hate

To this day, regardless of whether the message is a political one or whether the message is also meant to intimidate, the burning of a cross is a "symbol of hate." And while cross burning sometimes carries no intimidating message, at other times the intimidating message is the *only* message conveyed. . . . Indeed, as the cases of respondents Elliott and O'Mara indicate, individuals without Klan affiliation who wish to threaten or menace another person sometimes use cross burning because of this association between a burning cross and violence.

In sum, while a burning cross does not inevitably convey a message of intimidation, often the cross burner intends that the recipients of the message fear for their lives. And when a cross burning is used to intimidate, few if any messages are more powerful.

First Amendment Protections

The First Amendment, applicable to the States through the Fourteenth Amendment, provides that "Congress shall make no law . . . abridging the freedom of speech." The hallmark of the protection of free speech is to allow "free trade in ideas"—even ideas that the overwhelming majority of people might find distasteful or discomforting. . . .

The protections afforded by the First Amendment, however, are not absolute, and we have long recognized that the government may regulate certain categories of expression consistent with the Constitution. . . .

Thus, for example, a State may punish those words "which by their very utterance inflict injury or tend to incite an immediate breach of the peace" [*Chaplinsky v. New Hampshire*, 1942]. . . .

"True threats" encompass those statements where the speaker means to communicate a serious expression of an intent to commit an act of unlawful violence to a particular individual or group of individuals. . . . Intimidation in the constitutionally proscribable sense of the word is a type of true threat, where a speaker directs a threat to a person or group of persons with the intent of placing the victim in fear of bodily harm or death. Respondents do not contest that some cross burnings fit within this meaning of intimidating speech, and rightly so. The history of cross burning in this country shows that cross burning is often intimidating, intended to create a pervasive fear in victims that they are a target of violence. . . .

Some Content-Based Discrimination Permitted

The fact that cross burning is symbolic expression, however, does not resolve the constitutional question. The Supreme Court of Virginia relied upon *R.A.V. v. City of St. Paul* (1992), to conclude that once a statute discriminates on the basis of this type of content, the law is unconstitutional. We disagree.

In *R.A.V.*, we held that a local ordinance that banned certain symbolic conduct, including cross burning, when done with the knowledge that such conduct would "arouse anger, alarm or resentment in others on the basis of race, color, creed, religion or gender" was unconstitutional. We held that the ordinance did not pass constitutional muster because it discriminated on the basis of content by targeting only those individuals who "provoke violence" on a basis specified in the law. The ordinance did not cover "[t]hose who wish to use 'fighting words' in connection with other ideas to express hostility, for example, on the basis of political affiliation, union membership, or homosexuality." This content-based discrimination was unconstitutional because it allowed the city "to impose special prohibitions on those speakers who express views on disfavored subjects."

We did not hold in *R.A.V.* that the First Amendment prohibits *all* forms of content-based discrimination within a proscribable area of speech. Rather, we specifically stated that some types of content discrimination did not violate the First Amendment:

> "When the basis for the content discrimination consists entirely of the very reason the entire class of speech at issue is proscribable, no significant danger of idea or viewpoint discrimination exists. Such a reason, having been adjudged neutral enough to support exclusion of the entire class of speech from First Amendment protection, is also neutral enough to form the basis of distinction within the class. . . ."

Intent to Intimidate

Similarly, Virginia's statute does not run afoul of the First Amendment insofar as it bans cross burning with intent to intimidate. Unlike the statute at issue in *R.A.V.*, the Virginia statute does not single out for opprobrium [reproach] only that speech directed toward "one of the specified disfavored topics." It does not matter whether an individual burns a cross with intent to intimidate because of the victim's race, gender, or religion, or because of the victim's "political affiliation, union membership, or homosexuality." Moreover, as a factual matter it is not true that cross burners direct their intimidating conduct solely to racial or religious minorities. . . .

The First Amendment permits Virginia to outlaw cross burnings done with the intent to intimidate because burning a cross is a particularly virulent form of intimidation. Instead of prohibiting all intimidating messages, Virginia may choose to regulate this subset of intimidating messages in light of cross burning's long and pernicious history as a signal of impending violence. Thus, just as a State may regulate only that obscenity which is the most obscene due to its prurient content, so too may a State choose to prohibit only those forms of intimidation that are most likely to inspire fear of bodily harm. A ban on cross burning carried out with the intent to intimidate is fully consistent with our holding in *R.A.V.* and is proscribable under the First Amendment.

Statute Overbroad

The Supreme Court of Virginia ruled in the alternative that Virginia's cross-burning statute was unconstitutionally overbroad due to its provision stating that "[a]ny such burning of a cross shall be prima facie evidence of an intent to intimidate a person or group of persons." The Commonwealth added the prima facie provision to the statute in 1968. The court below did not reach whether this provision is severable from the rest of the cross-burning statute under Virginia law. . . .

The Supreme Court of Virginia has not ruled on the meaning of the prima facie evidence provision. It has, however, stated that "the act of burning a cross alone, with no evidence of intent to intimidate, will nonetheless suffice for arrest and prosecution and will insulate the Commonwealth from a motion to strike the evidence at the end of its case-in-chief. . . ."

The prima facie evidence provision, as interpreted by the jury instruction, renders the statute unconstitutional. . . . The prima facie evidence provision permits a jury to convict in every cross-burning case in which defendants exercise their constitutional right not to put on a defense. And even where a defendant like Black presents a defense, the prima facie evidence provision makes it more likely that the jury will find an intent to intimidate regardless of the particular facts of the case. The provision permits the Commonwealth to arrest, prosecute, and convict a person based solely on the fact of cross burning itself. . . .

Prima Facie Evidence

The act of burning a cross may mean that a person is engaging in constitutionally proscribable intimidation. But that same act may mean only that the person is engaged in core political speech. The prima facie evidence provision in this statute blurs the line between these two meanings of a burning cross. As interpreted by the jury instruction, the provision chills constitutionally protected political speech because of the possibility that a State will prosecute—and potentially convict—somebody engaging only in lawful political speech at the core of what the First Amendment is designed to protect.

As the history of cross burning indicates, a burning cross is not always intended to intimidate. Rather, sometimes the cross burning is a statement of ideology, a symbol of group solidarity. It is a ritual used at Klan gatherings, and it is used to represent the Klan itself. Thus, "[b]urning a cross at a political rally would almost certainty be protected expression" [*R.A.V. v. St. Paul*]. . . .

A Question of Intent

The prima facie provision makes no effort to distinguish among these different types of cross burnings. It does not distinguish between a cross burning done with the purpose of creating anger or resentment and a cross burning done with the purpose of threatening or intimidating a victim. It does not distinguish between a cross burning at a public rally or a cross burning on a neighbor's lawn. It does not treat the cross burning directed at an individual differently from the cross burning directed at a group of like-minded believers. It allows a jury to treat a cross burning on the property of another with the owner's acquiescence in the same manner as a cross burning on the property of another without the owner's permission. . . .

It may be true that a cross burning, even at a political rally, arouses a sense of anger or hatred among the vast majority of citizens who see a burning cross. But this sense of anger or hatred is not sufficient to ban all cross burnings. . . . The prima facie evidence provision in this case ignores all of the contextual factors that are necessary to decide whether a particular cross burning is intended to intimidate. The First Amendment does not permit such a shortcut.

> *"In our culture, cross burning has almost invariably meant lawlessness and understandably instills in its victims well-grounded fear of physical violence."*

Dissenting Opinion: All Cross Burnings Threaten Harm

Clarence Thomas

In Virginia v. Black et al., *the Court ruled that States could ban cross burning that was intended to intimidate. Although Clarence Thomas agrees with the majority decision upholding state bans on cross burning, he disagrees with the plurality opinion that invalidates the Virginia statute's prima facie evidence clause mandating that all cross burnings be considered a form of intimidation. In the following dissenting opinion, Thomas asserts that the history of cross burning, especially by the Ku Klux Klan, clearly demonstrates the threat of violence—not only for blacks, but also for racial minorities, Catholics, Jews, communists, members of labor unions, and any other group targeted by the Klan. In addition, Thomas claims the Virginia law prohibits conduct, not expression; therefore, since conduct—not expression—is addressed, the statute does not need to be analyzed in light of the First Amendment guarantee of freedom of speech. Clarence Thomas, a staunch conservative, was appointed to the Supreme Court in 1991 by President George H. W. Bush.*

Clarence Thomas, dissenting opinion, *Virginia v. Black et al.*, U.S. Supreme Court, 538 U.S. 343, in Legal Information Institute, Cornell University Law School, 2003.

In every culture, certain things acquire meaning well beyond what outsiders can comprehend. That goes for both the sacred and the profane. I believe that cross burning is the paradigmatic example of the latter.

Although I agree with the majority's conclusion that it is constitutionally permissible to "ban . . . cross burning carried out with intent to intimidate," I believe that the majority errs in imputing an expressive component to the activity in question. In my view, whatever expressive value cross burning has, the legislature simply wrote it out by banning only intimidating conduct undertaken by a particular means. A conclusion that the statute prohibiting cross burning with intent to intimidate sweeps beyond a prohibition on certain conduct into the zone of expression overlooks not only the words of the statute but also reality. . . .

The Brutal Methods of the Ku Klux Klan

To me, the majority's brief history of the Ku Klux Klan only reinforces this common understanding of the Klan as a terrorist organization, which, in its endeavor to intimidate, or even eliminate those its dislikes, uses the most brutal of methods.

Such methods typically include cross burning—"a tool for the intimidation and harassment of racial minorities, Catholics, Jews, communists, and any other groups hated by the Klan" [*Capitol Square Review and Advisory Bd. v. Pinette*, 1995]. For those not easily frightened, cross burning has been followed by more extreme measures, such as beatings and murder. . . .

But the perception that a burning cross is a threat and a precursor of worse things to come is not limited to blacks. Because the modern Klan expanded the list of its enemies beyond blacks and "radical[s]," to include Catholics, Jews, most immigrants, and labor unions, a burning cross is now widely viewed as a signal of impending terror and lawlessness.

I wholeheartedly agree with the observation made by the Commonwealth of Virginia that:

> "A white, conservative, middle-class Protestant, waking up at night to find a burning cross outside his home, will reasonably understand that someone is threatening him. His reaction is likely to be very different than if he were to find, say, a burning circle or square. In the latter case, he may call the fire department. In the former, he will probably call the police."

In our culture, cross burning has almost invariably meant lawlessness and understandably instills in its victims well-grounded fear of physical violence.

The Ku Klux Klan in Virginia

Virginia's experience has been no exception. In Virginia, though facing widespread opposition in 1920s, the KKK developed localized strength in the southeastern part of the State, where there were reports of scattered raids and floggings. Although the KKK was disbanded at the national level in 1944, a series of cross burnings in Virginia took place between 1949 and 1952. . . .

That in the early 1950s the people of Virginia viewed cross burning as creating an intolerable atmosphere of terror is not surprising: Although the cross took on some religious significance in the 1920s when the Klan became connected with certain southern white clergy, [according to W. Wade] by the postwar period it had reverted to its original function "as an instrument of intimidation. . . ."

Strengthening Delegate [Mills E. Jr.] Godwin's explanation [which states that "law and order in the state were impossible if organized groups could create fear by intimidation"], as well as my conclusion, that the legislature sought to criminalize terrorizing *conduct* is the fact that at the time the statute was enacted, racial segregation was not only the prevailing practice, but also the law in Virginia. And, just two years after the enactment of this statute, Virginia's General Assembly embarked on a campaign of "massive resistance" in response to *Brown v. Board of Education* (1954). . . .

It is simply beyond belief that, in passing the statute now under review, the Virginia legislature was concerned with anything but penalizing conduct it must have viewed as particularly vicious.

Accordingly, this statute prohibits only conduct, not expression. And, just as one cannot burn down someone's house to make a political point and then seek refuge in the First Amendment, those who hate cannot terrorize and intimidate to make their point. In light of my conclusion that the statute here addresses only conduct, there is no need to analyze it under any of our First Amendment tests. . . .

The Question of Intimidation

The plurality, however, is troubled by the presumption because this is a First Amendment case. The plurality laments the fate of an innocent cross-burner who burns a cross, but does so without an intent to intimidate. The plurality fears the chill on expression because, according to the plurality, the inference permits "the Commonwealth to arrest, prosecute and convict a person based solely on the fact of cross burning itself. . . ."

Moreover, even in the First Amendment context, the Court has upheld such regulations where conduct that initially appears culpable, ultimately results in dismissed charges. A regulation of pornography is one such example. While possession of child pornography is illegal, possession of adult pornography, as long as it is not obscene, is allowed. As a result, those pornographers trafficking in images of adults who look like minors, may be not only deterred but also arrested and prosecuted for possessing what a jury might find to be legal materials. This "chilling" effect has not, however, been a cause for grave concern with respect to overbreadth of such statutes among the members of this Court.

That the First Amendment gives way to other interests is not a remarkable proposition. What is remarkable is that, under the plurality's analysis, the determination of whether an interest is sufficiently compelling depends not on the harm a regulation in question seeks to prevent, but on the area of society at which it aims. . . . The plurality strikes down the statute because one day an individual might wish to burn a cross, but might do so without an intent to intimidate anyone. That cross burning subjects its targets, and, sometimes, an unintended audience, to extreme emotional distress, and is virtually never viewed merely as "unwanted communication," but rather, as a physical threat, is of no concern to the plurality. Henceforth, under the plurality's view, physical safety will be valued less than the right to be free from unwanted communications.

Because I would uphold the validity of this statute, I respectfully dissent.

"Tthe Supreme Court found that one form of vile expression, cross-burning, falls outside the First Amendment's umbrella of protection, if the state can prove that it was done with the intent to intimidate."

The Full Effect of *Virginia v. Black* Remains To Be Seen

Tony Mauro

Virginia v. Black *tested the constitutionality of Virginia's ban on cross burning. The Supreme Court held that states may ban cross burning that is intended to intimidate. In the following essay Tony Mauro declares that predicting the impact of the Court's 6–3 decision in* Virginia v. Black *is impossible, given the fractured decision that included combinations of concurrences and dissents among the Justices. In the majority opinion, Justice Sandra Day O'Connor proclaimed that the broad protection of the First Amendment does not extend to cross burning if it is meant to intimidate, citing the long and lurid history of cross burning and the violence and evil associated with it. Mauro reports that First Amendment advocates hope the decision is limited to one classification of expression—cross burning—and will not lead to attempts by ardent lawmakers to outlaw other forms of speech, such as swastikas or flag burning. Mauro stresses O'Connor's insistence that forms of expression not protected by the freedom of speech guarantee must be "true threats" of violence. Tony Mauro, is the Supreme Court correspondent for* Legal Times, *American Lawyer Media, law.com, and the First Amendment Center.*

Tony Mauro, "Too Early to Know Full Effect of Cross-Burning Ruling," First Amendment Center, April 8, 2003. Reproduced by permission.

One hallmark of the Supreme Court's First Amendment jurisprudence is the protection of the right of individuals to express themselves in controversial—even vile and objectionable—ways.

Yesterday [April 7, 2003], the Supreme Court found that one form of vile expression, cross-burning, falls outside the First Amendment's umbrella of protection, if the state can prove that it was done with the intent to intimidate.

"When a cross burning is used to intimidate, few if any messages are more powerful," wrote Justice Sandra Day O'Connor for a majority in *Virginia v. Black.*

As a result, how much of a dent did the Court's [6–3] decision in *Virginia v. Black* make in its First Amendment edifice?

"Too early to tell" seems to be the best answer from an early reading of the multifaceted, highly fractured opinion.

Dissent Within the Court

The three justices who dissented on mainly First Amendment grounds said the Virginia cross-burning law upheld by the Court's majority amounted to impermissible content discrimination, because it "selects a symbol with particular content from the field of all proscribable expression meant to intimidate." By doing so, it threatens to suppress speech, not just intimidation, wrote Justice David Souter. "Even when the symbolic act is meant to terrify, a burning cross may carry a further, ideological message of white, Protestant supremacy."

And the fatal flaw in the statute is not cured, Souter went on to say, by the majority's agreement that one provision of the Virginia statute should be struck down. That provision says that the very act of cross-burning amounts to "prima facie evidence of an intent to intimidate." In other words, under that part of the law, even cross-burning that is the equivalent of political speech—at an entirely legal Ku Klux Klan rally, for example—is presumed to be intimidating and therefore illegal.

Justices Anthony Kennedy and Ruth Bader Ginsburg joined Souter in his dissent, which invoked the Court's 1992 decision striking down another cross-burning statute, in *R.A.V. v. City of St. Paul.*

Threat of Intimidation Required

But to others, the Court's decision to strike down the presumption part of the Virginia statute, plus its recitation of the long, unique history of cross-burning, may have limited its impact, creating a "category of one" that converts cross-burning into a special form of speech that, like obscenity, can be banned. To use yesterday's precedent as a justification for banning other kinds of vile speech, the hope is, a similar history would have to be shown, and there would have to be some ability for the accused person to prove he or she did not intend to intimidate.

Another hopeful sign for First Amendment advocates, found deep in O'Connor's majority opinion, is that she may have narrowed the category of "true threats" that can be prohibited without violating the First Amendment. "True threats encompass those statements where the speaker means to communicate a serious expression of an intent to commit an act of unlawful violence to a particular individual or group of individuals," O'Connor wrote. In past rulings, the Court has required a more objective test for true threats, one that looks at how a reasonable person might perceive the threat. Focusing instead on what the speaker "means to communicate" may make prosecutions more difficult.

The First Amendment and the Presumption Provision

Seven justices—all but Antonin Scalia and Clarence Thomas—agreed that the presumption provision violates the First Amendment.

"The prima facie evidence provision in this case ignores all of the contextual factors that are necessary to decide whether a particular cross burning is intended to intimidate," wrote Justice Sandra Day O'Connor for the majority. "The First Amendment does not permit such a shortcut."

Justice Clarence Thomas, the Court's only African American member, dissented, arguing that the First Amendment was not even a factor in evaluating the statute, which he found to be entirely constitutional.

"This statute prohibits only conduct, not expression," wrote Thomas. "Just as one cannot burn down someone's house to make a political point and then seek refuge in the First Amendment, those who hate cannot terrorize and intimidate to make their point."

Thomas, in his 11 years on the bench, has become viewed as one of the strongest First Amendment defenders on the Court. Because of the special significance of cross-burning in his own upbringing in segregated Georgia, Thomas apparently felt he had to remove the First Amendment from the analysis in order to uphold the law.

Reach of Decision a Concern

First Amendment advocates expressed concern that yesterday's ruling could lead overzealous legislators to use the intimidation rationale to outlaw other forms of controversial speech, from swastikas to flag-burning.

A current case pending before the Court, *American Coalition of Life Activists v. Planned Parenthood of the Columbia/Willamette*, No. 02-563, involves the so-called Nuremberg Files anti-abortion Web site that lists names and addresses of abortion providers. That site has been challenged as an impermissible threat that should not be protected by the First Amendment.

"Our concern is how much the language in the decision would lend itself to being used in other contexts," said Joshua Wheeler, lawyer at the Thomas Jefferson Center for the Protection of Free Expression in Charlottesville, VA, which filed a brief against the Virginia cross-burning law. "Even if the Court intended its ruling to be limited to cross burning, the potential always exists for legislators to go beyond that."

Cross Burning a Unique Threat

Virginia Attorney General Jerry Kilgore commented, "A burning cross is a symbol like no other. It doesn't just say, 'We don't like you.' The message is, 'We are going to do you harm.'"

Kent Scheidegger, legal director of the Criminal Justice Legal Foundation, called the ruling "a victory for race relations in America. . . . In our history, burning a cross on someone's front yard is a threat which is not protected by the First Amendment."

The Court fashioned its ruling by treating the case of Barry Black differently from the case of Richard Elliott and Jonathan O'Mara, all of whom had been arrested and charged in different cross-burning incidents.

Black was arrested under the Virginia law in 1998 after burning a cross in an open field in connection with a Ku Klux Klan rally. Elliott and O'Mara, by contrast, were arrested in a separate incident in which they burned a cross on the lawn of Elliott's African American neighbor.

The Virginia Supreme Court struck down the law as it applied to all three defendants, finding that it was "analytically indistinguishable" from the statute invalidated in *R.A.V.*

But Justice O'Connor found the law objectionable mainly in the case of Black, a Klan leader. Applying the law's presumption to him, O'Connor suggested, deprived him of the ability to make a defense that he was "engaged in core political speech."

As for Elliott and O'Mara, O'Connor said the presumption was never invoked. O'Mara pleaded guilty, and a jury found Elliott guilty without being instructed by the judge on the presumption aspect of the law.

Jurisdictions with anti-cross-burning laws similar to Virginia's include California, Connecticut, Delaware, Florida, Georgia, Idaho, Montana, North Carolina, South Carolina, South Dakota, Vermont, Washington, and the District of Columbia.

> *"Cross burning is uniquely terrifying to the black community."*

Virginia v. Black Did Not Go Far Enough to Protect Against Cross Burnings

Bruce Fein

Though attorney Bruce Fein agrees with the majority ruling in Virginia v. Black *that cross burning meant to intimidate does not violate the First Amendment right of free speech, in this essay he states that the Court erred in deciding that a law could not presume intent to intimidate without examining motive in each case. In the decision handed down by Justice Sandra Day O'Connor, a cross burning may not threaten violence in every situation. Fein concludes cross burnings that threaten and intimidate blacks could still receive First Amendment protection under the plurality decision and concludes that cross burning is never without some intent to intimidate. Bruce Fein is the founding partner of the Washington, D.C., law firm, Fein & Fein.*

The United States Supreme Court correctly concluded in *Virginia v. Black* [April 7, 2003] that cross burning with an intent to intimidate was unprotected by the First Amendment; but it erred by insisting that a hypothetical possibility of prosecuting a benevolent cross burner prohibited a legal presumption that a burning, simpliciter [Latin for simply; frankly] could prove a malignant intent. As Justice Samuel Miller lectured in *United States v. Lee* [1882]: "Hypothetical cases of great evils may be suggested by a particularly fruitful imagination in regard to almost every law upon which depend the rights of the individual or of the government, and if the existence of laws is to depend upon the capacity to withstand such criticism, the whole fabric of the law must fail."

Cross burning is uniquely terrifying to the black community. By legend and experience, burning a cross came to be understood as the signature of the Ku Klux Klan's intent to retaliate against any black who balked at white supremacy. Indeed, as the Nazi swastika is to the Jews, cross burnings are to blacks a frightening symbol of threatened death and destruction that chills the heart and obsesses the mind. History speaks volumes.

Born in 1866 in Pulaski, Tenn., the Klan commenced to terrorize Freedmen during Reconstruction through whippings, murder and threatened stake burnings. After a period of dormancy, a second Klan emerged in 1905 sporting the same odious agenda and employing the same loathsome tactics. By September 1921, the *New York World Newspaper* documented 152 acts of Klan violence, including 4 murders, 41 floggings, and 27 tar-and-featherings.

The Terror of Cross Burnings

In Miami in 1941, the Klan burned four crosses abutting a proposed housing project, declaring, "We are here to keep n-----s out of your town. . . ." Klan violence escalated into bombings, beatings, shootings, stabbings, and mutilations to oppose the civil rights movement of the 1950s and 1960s. It is virtually inconceivable in light of this past that a black could either witness or learn of a cross burning without paralyzing trauma or fright. The narrative of a lower court opinion in 1991 is gripping: "After the mother saw the burning cross, she was crying on her knees in the living room. [She] felt feelings of frustration and intimidation and feared for her husband's life. She testified what the burning cross symbolized to her as a black American: 'murder, hanging, rape, lynching. Just about anything bad that you can name. It is the worst thing that can happen to a person.' Mr. Heisser told the probation officer that at the time of the occurrence, if the family did not leave, he believed someone would return to commit murder. . . . Seven months after the incident, the family still lived in fear. . . . This is a reaction reasonably to be anticipated from this criminal conduct."

The Jubilee family, victimized by a cross burning at their home implicated in *Virginia v. Black*, was similarly pulsated with fright. As reported in *The Washington Post*, James, the father, paced the halls of his Virginia Beach house at night with his gun nearby. His wife, Susan, ceased early-morning walks and recalled movie scenes featuring KKK rallies. Their 8-year old boy was given security protection during recess. Susan explained the psychology at work: "We didn't know who did it. We didn't know if it was an organized hate group or just kids. We didn't know if this was a warning that we had to get out or they were going to firebomb our house in the middle of the night." And James elaborated: "I had never, ever in my life encountered anything of the sort. All I knew, from what I had been told, is that when something like that occurred, something worse was coming."

The First Amendment Could Still Protect Cross Burning

Writing for the Court in *Virginia v. Black*, Justice Sandra Day O'Connor thus sensibly held that Virginia's prohibition of cross burning with an "intent to intimidate a person or group of persons" was undisturbing to the First Amendment. Threats to commit mayhem have never enjoyed a free speech sanctuary. And Virginia's singling out cross burnings from other conduct intending to intimidate was justified because its evils uniquely inflame community passions and petrify an entire race.

Justice O'Connor struck down, nevertheless, a portion of the statute that permitted juries to find an intent to intimidate from the fact of cross burning alone. She worried that the cross burnings in the movie *Mississippi Burning* and the stage adaptation of Sir Walter Scott's "The Lady of the Lake" were not ill-motivated, yet might be vulnerable to prosecution. But to believe that a jury would ever infer an intent to intimidate in such circumstances is to hallucinate.

Question of Intent Troublesome

Justice O'Connor also maintained that cross burnings that torment the black community and teach subjugation of the black race without intending to intimidate deserve First Amendment protection. But as Justice Clarence Thomas countered in a dissenting opinion, "Considering the horrific effect cross burning has on its victims, it is also reasonable to presume an intent to intimidate from the act itself." Justice O'Connor also enlisted the example of Nazi Germany as demonstrating the urgency of safeguarding the most squalid and bigoted ideas.

But that turns history on its head. Adolf Hitler and the Nazis exploited hate speech during the Weimar Republic to poison the minds of the German electorate and to capture the Reichstag. And then came the end of free speech and the Jews. Cross burners in the United States, whether or not they intend to intimidate, aim at a similar grisly chapter for blacks and speech celebrating equal rights. Why should the risk that they might succeed, no matter how tiny, be accepted when cross burnings make no contribution to civilized discourse?

Organizations to Contact

The editors have compiled the following list of organizations concerned with the issues debated in this book. The descriptions are derived from materials provided by the organizations. All have publications or information available for interested readers. The list was compiled on the date of publication of the present volume; the information provided here may change. Be aware that many organizations take several weeks or longer to respond to inquiries, so allow as much time as possible.

American-Arab Anti-Discrimination Committee (ADC)
4201 Connecticut Avenue, Washington, DC 20008
(202) 244-2990 • fax: (202) 244-3196
e-mail: adc@adc.org
Web site: www.adc.org

The American-Arab Anti-Discrimination Committee (ADC) is a civil rights organization committed to combating discrimination and promoting intercultural awareness of people of Arab heritage. Through a network of international chapters, the group works to protect Arab American civil rights. The committee publishes the newsletter *ADC Times* and a yearly report summarizing incidents of hate crimes, defamation, and discrimination against Arab Americans.

American Civil Liberties Union (ACLU)
125 Broad Street, 17th Floor, New York, NY 10004
(212) 607-3300 • fax: (212) 607-3318
Web site: www.aclu.org

The mission of the American Civil Liberties Union (ACLU) is to preserve the guarantees and protections of the Bill of Rights, other Amendments, and other rights providing equal protection and equal treatment under the law. The ACLU handles nearly six thousand court cases annually, actively tracks courts and legislatures, and issues a series of *ACLU Briefing Reports* on every major civil rights topic, including hate crimes.

American Psychological Association (APA)
Office of Public Affairs, Washington, DC 20002-4242
(202) 336-5700 • fax: (202) 336-5708
Web site: www.apa.org

The American Psychological Association (APA) seeks to inform both professionals and laymen of the myriad psychological issues that naturally include the perpetrators and victims of hate crimes. The association strives to encourage communities to promote educational programs intent on dispelling minority stereotypes, reducing hostility between groups, and encouraging broader intercultural appreciation and understanding. The group publishes the *CRS Bulletin*, APA Online, books, children's books, *Position Papers*, and journals.

Anti-Defamation League (ADL)
823 United Nations Plaza, New York, NY 10017
(212) 490-2525
Web site: www.adl.org

Founded in 1913, the Anti-Defamation League (ADL) is the world's leading organization fighting anti-Semitism through projects and services that counteract hate crimes, bigotry, and racism. The group also monitors hate groups, particularly on the Internet. Its many publications include books, surveys, and frequent press releases on various civil rights topics including hate crimes, such as, *Hate on the World Wide Web*.

Aryan Nations
Church of Jesus Christ Christian, Hayden, ID 83835
(208) 772-2408
Web site: www.twelvearyannations.com

Aryan Nations and the Church of Jesus Christ Christian believe that whites are God's chosen people, nonwhites lack souls, and Jews are the children of Satan. It publishes the *Aryan Nation Newsletter* and pamphlets such as *New World Order in North America*, *Aryan Warriors Stand*, and *Know Your Enemies*.

Federal Bureau of Investigation (FBI)
J. Edgar Hoover Building, Washington, DC 20535
(202) 324-3000
Web site: www.fbi.gov

The Federal Bureau of Investigation (FBI) is the U.S. government's lead agency for investigating violations of federal civil rights laws. For the FBI, investigating hate crimes—that is, attacks motivated by bias—is their top civil rights priority because of the extensive toll it takes on families and communities. Reports and publications cover the history and the current Strategic Plan, as well as terrorism, hate crime, violent crime, and terrorism. *Uniform Crime Reports* address U.S. crime in general and hate crime statistics in particular.

First Amendment Center
First Amendment Center at Vanderbilt University
Nashville, TN 37212
(615) 727-1600 • fax: (615) 727-1319
Web site: www.firstamendmentcenter.org

The First Amendment Center strives to protect and preserve First Amendment freedoms through education and information. The nonpartisan center serves as a forum for the study and exploration of issues involving freedom of expression, including freedom of speech, press, and religion. The site provides authoritative sources of news, information, and commentary on First Amendment issues, including hate speech. Publications include *First Reports* and *State of the First Amendment* reports. The site features news from the Associated Press, staff writers, and guest articles and editorials.

Leadership Conference on Civil Rights (LCCR)
1629 K Street NW, 10th Floor, Washington, DC 20006
(202) 466-3311
Web site: www.civilrights.org

Founded in 1950, the Leadership Conference on Civil Rights (LCCR) is the premier civil rights coalition, orchestrating the national legislative campaign on behalf of every major civil rights law since 1957. The LCCR provides relevant, breaking news and information on civil rights concerns, including hate crimes. The coalition publishes e-mail newsletters, reports, curricula, and a quarterly publication, the *Civil Rights Monitor.*

National Alliance
PO Box 90, Hillsboro, WV 24946
(304) 653-4600
Web site: www.natvan.com

The National Alliance believes that in comparison to all other races, the white race is superior in intelligence, ability, and creativity. It argues that all whites have an obligation to fight for the creation of a white nation that is free of non-Aryan influence. It publishes the newsletter *Free Speech* and the magazine *National Vanguard.*

National Association for the Advancement of Colored People (NAACP)
4805 Mt. Hope Drive, Baltimore, MD 21215
(877) 622-2798
Web site: www.naacp.org

The National Association for the Advancement of Colored People (NAACP) is the oldest and largest civil rights organization in the United States. Its principal objectives are to achieve equal rights, eliminate racial prejudice, and promote tolerance, thereby reducing racist hate crimes. The NAACP publishes a variety of newsletters, books, and pamphlets, as well as the magazine *Crisis.*

National Gay and Lesbian Task Force (NGLTF)
1700 Kalorama Road NW, Washington, DC 20009
(202) 332-6483 • fax: (202) 332-0207
Web site: www.ngltf.org

As a civil rights organization, the National Gay and Lesbian Task Force (NGLTF) fights bigotry and violence against gays and lesbians. It sponsors conferences and organizes local groups to promote civil rights legislation for gays and lesbians. It publishes the monthly *Eye on Equality* column and distributes reports, fact sheets, and bibliographies on antigay violent hate crimes.

National Organization for Women (NOW)
1100 H Street NW, 3rd Floor, Washington, DC 20005
(202) 628-8669 • fax: (202) 785-8576
Web site: www.now.org

Stressing discrimination and gender-bias, the National Organization for Women (NOW) promotes federal and state legislation that addresses the prevalence of gender-motivated hate crimes. Despite gains made by the civil rights and women's rights movements, NOW works to establish equality for all women. Activities include creating legal clinics, forming meetings and rallies, filing petitions, issuing press releases, and lobbying legislators. NOW publishes the *National NOW Times*.

For Further Research

Books

Donald Altschiller, *Hate Crimes: A Reference Handbook*. Santa Barbara, CA: ABC-CLIO, 2005.

Kathleen Blee, *Inside Organized Racism: Women in the Hate Movement*. Berkeley: University of California Press, 2002.

Colin Flint, *Spaces of Hate: Geographies of Discrimination and Intolerance in the U.S.A.* New York: Routledge, 2004.

Phyllis B. Gerstenfeld and Diana R. Grant, eds., *Crimes of Hate: Selected Readings*. Thousand Oaks, CA: 2004.

Michael J. Klarman, *From Jim Crow to Civil Rights: The Supreme Court and the Struggle for Racial Equality*. New York: Oxford University Press, 2004.

Frederick M. Lawrence, *Punishing Hate: Bias Crimes Under American Law*. Cambridge, MA: Harvard University Press, 1999.

Jack Levin and Jack McDevitt, *Hate Crimes Revisited: America's War Against Those Who Are Different*. Boulder, CO: Westview Press, 2002.

Martha Minow, *Breaking the Cycles of Hatred: Memory, Law, and Repair*. Princeton, NJ: Princeton University Press, 2002.

David A. Neiwert, *Death on the Fourth of July: The Story of a Killing, a Trial, and Hate Crimes in America*. New York: Palgrave Macmillan, 2004.

Barbara Perry, *In the Name of Hate: Understanding Hate Crimes*. New York: Routledge, 2001.

Chester L. Quarles, *The Ku Klux Klan and Related American Racialist and Antisemitic Groups: A History and Analysis*. Jefferson, NC: McFarland, 1999.

Ishmael Reed, *Another Day at the Front: Dispatches from the Race War*. New York: Basic Books, 2003.

Michael R. Ronczkowski, *Terrorism and Organized Hate Crime: Intelligence Gathering, Analysis and Investigations*. 2nd ed. New York: Routledge, 2006.

Mamie Till-Mobley, *Death of Innocence: The Story of the Hate Crime That Changed America*. New York: Random House, 2003.

Christopher Waldrep, *Racial Violence on Trial: A Handbook with Cases, Laws, and Documents*. Santa Barbara, CA: ABC-CLIO, 2001.

Samuel Walker, *Hate Speech: The History of an American Controversy*. Lincoln: University of Nebraska Press, 1994.

Michael Welch, *Scapegoats of September 11th: Hate Crimes and State Crimes in the War on Terror*. New Brunswick, NJ: Rutgers University Press, 2006.

Periodicals

Anthony V. Alfieri, "Retrying Race," *Michigan Law Review*, vol. 101, no. 5, March 2005.

Sara Sun Beale, "Federalizing Hate Crimes: Symbolic Politics, Expressive Law, or Tool for Criminal Enforcement," *Boston University Law Review*, 2000.

Marisol Bello, "'Jena 6' Case in La. Spurs Copycats; In Almost All of a Dozen Racial Incidents Since, Nooses Were Left at Scene," *USA Today*, October 10, 2007.

Rebekka S. Bonner, "Reconceptualizing VAWA's 'Animus' for Rape in States' Emerging Post-VAWA Civil Rights Legislation," *Yale Law Journal*, vol. 111, no. 6, April 2002.

Michael Brick, "To Commit a Hate Crime, Must the Criminal Truly Hate the Victim?" *New York Times*, June 20, 2007.

Amy Doolittle, "Criminalized Thoughts?" *Washington Times*, December 29, 2004.

Ryken Grattet and Valerie Jenness, "Criminology: Examining the Boundaries of Hate Crime Law: Disabilities and the 'Dilemma of Difference,'" *Journal of Criminal Law and Criminology*, vol. 91, Spring 2001.

Eun Hee Han, "Hate Crimes and Hate Speech," *Georgetown Journal of Gender and the Law*, vol. 7, 2006.

Stephen Henderson, "*Brown* Case Set Equal-Rights Progress in Motion; The Landmark Ruling Affirmed That the High Court Could Protect Liberties in Issues Even Beyond Race," *Philadelphia Inquirer*, May 23, 2004.

Carl Hulse, "Congressional Maneuvering Dooms Hate Crimes Measure," *New York Times*, December 7, 2007.

David A. Kaplan and Daniel Klaidman, "A Battle, Not the War," *Newsweek*, June 3, 1996.

Kristin M. Jasket, "Racists, Skinheads and Gay-Bashers Beware: Congress Joins the Battle Against Hate Crimes by Proposing the Hate Crimes Prevention Act of 1999," *Seton Hall Legislative Journal*, vol. 24, 2000.

Edward M. Kennedy and John Lewis, "We Must Not Tolerate Hate Crimes," *Christian Science Monitor*, November 30, 2007.

Joyce King, "Hate Crime Laws Lack Clout, Funds," *USA Today*, October 5, 2007.

Terry A. Maroney, "The Struggle Against Hate Crime: Movement at a Crossroads," *New York Late Review*, vol. 73, 1998.

Stephen Russell Martin II, "Establishing the Constitutional Use of Bias-Inspired Beliefs and Expressions in Penalty

Enhancement for Hate Crimes: *Wisconsin v. Mitchell*," *Creighton Law Review*, vol. 27, February 1994.

Petal Nevella Modeste, "Race Hate Speech: The Pervasive Badge of Slavery Mocks the Thirteenth Amendment," *Howard Law Journal*, vol. 44, 2001.

Gregory R. Nearpass, "The Overlooked Constitutional Objection and Practical Concerns to Penalty-Enhancement Provisions of Hate Crime Legislation," *Albany Law Review*, vol. 66, no. 2, Winter 2002.

Edward Rothstein, "Hate Crimes: What Is Gained When Forbidden Acts Become Forbidden Beliefs?" *New York Times*, September 19, 2005.

William B. Rubenstein, "The Real Story of U.S. Hate Crime Statistics: An Empirical Analysis," *Tulane Late Review*, vol. 78, March 2004.

Troy A. Scotting, "Hate Crimes and the Need for Stronger Federal Legislation," *Akron Late Review*, vol. 34, 2001.

Alyssa Shenk, "Victim-Offender Mediation: The Road to Repairing Hate Crime Injustice," *Ohio State Journal of Dispute Resolution*, vol. 17, 2001.

Suzanne Sidun, "An End to the Violence: Justifying Gender as a 'Particular Social Group,'" *Pepperdine Law Review*, vol. 28, 2000.

Gordon H. Smith, "Nationally: Why Hate Crimes Are Different," *Washington Post*, June 19, 2000.

Andrew E. Taslitz, "Free Speech, and the Contract of Mutual Indifference," *Boston Late Review*, vol. 80, 2000.

George F. Will, "A Bustling Hate-Crime Industry," *Washington Post*, May 13, 2007.

Index

G

H

W